Teaching With Favorite
READ-ALOUDS
— in Kindergarten —

50 Must-Have Books with Lessons and Activities That Build Skills in Vocabulary, Comprehension, and More

By Susan Lunsford

New York • Toronto • London • Auckland • Sydney
Mexico City • New Delhi • Hong Kong • Buenos Aires

Teaching
Resources

DEDICATION

For Ryan & Maddie

And all the children who helped me with this book, especially

Mrs. Dobash's hard-working kindergartners.

Here's to happy kindergarten memories!

To Brad:

For 20 years of love, support, encouragement,

And, yes, Starbucks, too;

Thanks for turning so many dreams into reality.

For Joanna and Sarah,

Thank you for your guidance and support.

Cover design by Josuè Castilleja

Cover photograph by James Levin

Interior Design by LDL Designs, based on a design by Sarah Morrow

Interior illustrations by Sharon Holm

ISBN 0-439-40417-7

Printed in the U.S.A.

5 6 7 8 9 10   40   10 09 08 07

CONTENTS

"Fresh" Books Make
Kindergarten Memories

It's Library Day for kindergarten. I overhear the librarian giving suggestions to one very bookish little girl named Jocelyn.

"I want a 'fresh' book, one I've never read before," Jocelyn demands.

"Have you read all the Eric Carle books?" the librarian asks.

"All of them."

"How about *Olivia*?"

"We read that one a lot."

"The Max and Ruby books by Rosemary Wells are fun."

"I own all the Max and Ruby books."

"*The Napping House*?"

"Yes, that's one of my favorites. My dog chewed the cover."

"*Angelina Ballerina*?"

Jocelyn nods her head. "Yes. I got that one for my birthday. From Grandma. I'm a dancer, you know."

This back and forth continues a few more minutes until the librarian walks to her desk. She reaches into a box and pulls a book from the just-arrived-and-not-on-the-shelves-yet books. *"I'm Gonna Like Me: Letting Off a Little Self-Esteem?"* the librarian asks; she glances at me, lowers her voice and adds, "Not that you seem to be lacking in the self-esteem department."

Jocelyn's face lights up. "That girl on the cover looks like me! Is it brand new? Can I have it?"

The librarian smiles triumphantly. "It's hot off the press, nice and 'fresh.' I'll give it a bar code, and it's yours for the week."

From my eavesdropping, I learned that Jocelyn knows her books. She has an enviable collection, identifies her favorites, rereads them, and relates to the characters. Perhaps most impressive, she loves books. I watch her dancing with anticipation at the checkout counter. Book in hand, she heads to a table and begins poring over the pictures in *I'm Gonna Like Me*.

As I watch Jocelyn reading her "fresh" book, I replay her conversation with the librarian and go over my mental list of 50 must-have books for kindergarten. I smile, thinking that this list of books would meet with Jocelyn's approval. Each of the books will stand up to numerous rereadings, and is given a "fresh" twist with a follow-up book-based activity.

Read-alouds are a terrific way to introduce, model, and reinforce key reading skills and strategies. With memorable first-book experiences like the ones presented on the following pages, children look forward to read-aloud time each day and are motivated to want to learn to read. By incorporating phonetic and structural analysis, picture and meaning clues, and other pre-reading basics, the activities in this book will further inspire your students to get ready to read. Kindergarten teachers, and the Jocelyns of the world and their classmates, have the opportunity to make read-aloud memories every day. These memories made in kindergarten can start a love of reading that lasts a lifetime.

A Few Words About the Read-Aloud and Rich Vocabulary Connection

It's no surprise that by their senior year, students at the top of their class know about four times as many words as their lower performing classmates. "Most chilling, however," write Beck, McKeown, and Kucan in *Bringing Words to Life* (pages 1–2), "is the finding that once established, such differences appear difficult to ameliorate. This is clearly very bad news!"

The good news is that implementing effective vocabulary instruction has become a priority in elementary schools. Techniques for providing the most effective and meaningful vocabulary instruction have also been identified. For kindergarten teachers, the most appropriate place to begin is with a daily read-aloud, which gives the opportunity to teach one or two new words. Read-aloud time will provide a wealth of vocabulary words in meaningful contexts over the course of the school year.

In the pages of my book, I highlight one or more words from each of the 50 must-have read-aloud books. Activities and direct examples from my classroom illustrate how to best present words from trade books to help kindergarteners commit new word knowledge to memory and to apply these newly discovered words in new situations.

When sharing a wordless picture book, look for a prevailing theme or level-appropriate word to highlight for vocabulary instruction. In *A Boy, a Dog and a Frog*, for example, *frustration* is introduced as a rich vocabulary word. The word and definition are reinforced in future "retellings" of the story.

Chapter 1:
Meet Memorable Characters
10 Must-Have Books for Reinforcing Reading Readiness Skills

Chapter Learning Goals:
* understanding that print conveys meaning and is organized
* developing phonemic awareness
* reinforcing beginning letter sounds and letter recognition
* using phonetic analysis to decode unknown words
* using picture and other meaning clues to decode unknown words
* reading level-appropriate sight words
* strengthening oral language skills
* exploring rhyming words in the context of rhyming books
* enjoying great books with memorable characters

A book-based kindergarten class is filled with characters—book characters, that is. A couple of hard working mice, a polar bear, some alphabears, and a cat in a hat are just a few of the memorable friends that will make learning to read more enjoyable. Share each book for read-aloud, and then use the characters and their antics to reinforce skills and strategies of the reading process.

Explore rhyming words with *The Cat in the Hat* by Dr. Seuss, who is an expert rhyming word-smith. Hone letter-sound relationships with *Polar Bear, Polar Bear, What Do You Hear?* Don your hard hats, and construct picture dictionaries with a hardworking mouse in *Alphabet under Construction*. Identify words for treats from *A* to *Z* in the midst of *Mouse Mess*, and play some more with the alphabet and food while taste-testing *Eating the Alphabet: Fruits and Vegetables from A to Z.*

Challenge students to identify the first names on the pages of *Alphabears*, and learn everything about sound-spelling as *Olivia Saves the Circus.* Spotlight students' acts of bravery with inspiration from *Sheila Rae, the Brave.* Meet *The Cookie-Store Cat,* and then explore letter-sound relations while icing cookie cats, gingerbread men, puppies, and more. Hear and see how rhyming words work as you listen to *Top Cat* purr in his coat of fur.

10 Must-Have Books for Reinforcing Reading Readiness Skills

The Cat in the Hat by Dr. Seuss

Polar Bear, Polar Bear, What Do You Hear? by Bill Martin Jr. and John Archambault

Alphabet under Construction by Denise Fleming

Mouse Mess by Linnea Riley

Eating the Alphabet: Fruits and Vegetables from A to Z by Lois Ehlert

Alphabears by Kathleen Hague

Olivia Saves the Circus by Ian Falconer

Sheila Rae, the Brave by Kevin Henkes

The Cookie-Store Cat by Cynthia Rylant

Top Cat by Lois Ehlert

The Cat in the Hat

by Dr. Seuss

LEARNING ABOUT Rhyming Words

"I know it is wet
And the sun is not sunny.
But we can have
Lots of good fun that is funny!"
"I know some good games we could play,"
Said the cat.
"I know some new tricks,"
Said the Cat in the Hat.

— From *The Cat in the Hat*, pages 7–8

Our *Cat in the Hat* game

Let this dapper cat give your class a lot of good fun that is funny with a word study game that sharpens reading skills from early prereaders to solid beginning readers.

While some students will identify rhyming words because they sound alike, others will identify rhyming words because they look alike as well. The impact of the rhyming word concept for the kindergarten set is the realization that being able to read one word like *cat* empowers them to read a whole list of other words like *hat, bat, sat, rat,* and *mat*—just by changing one letter. This change-a-letter rhyming word technique builds confidence and helps young readers tackle words in a playful way.

Rich Vocabulary

tame *adj.* easy to handle (not wild)

Teaching With Favorite Read-Alouds in Kindergarten

In the mini-lesson that follows, kindergartners learn a few alphabet tricks from *The Cat in the Hat*. To prepare for the lesson, fill a shoebox with magnetic letters from *A* to *Z*, copy the note below, and tape it to the lid.

> *Please look in this box*
> *From Thing One and Thing Two,*
> *You'll find a fun game*
> *Of learning-to-read clues.*
>
> *Just twenty-six alphabet letters to learn,*
> *All of the words in the world, any found in a book,*
> *Are made with these twenty-six letters—*
> *Just look!*
>
> *Put these letters in order,*
> *C with A-T makes CAT.*
> *Replace C with H,*
> *Now the CAT is a HAT.*
>
> *I know it's a challenge,*
> *but it can be funny,*
> *And learning to read*
> *Will make your days sunny.*
>
> *I'm the Cat in the Hat,*
> *And I'm here to say*
> *Reading is fun!*
> *Start learning today.*

After reading aloud this classic book to your students, display the shoebox and let the lesson begin. Here's a sample of how I get things rolling in my classroom.

Mrs. L.:	I found this box sitting on my desk when I came to school today. *(I read aloud the note.)*
Tara:	It's from the Cat in the Hat.
Jordan:	How did he sneak into our classroom?
Mrs. L.:	It's hard to say. What do you think is in the box?
Jordan:	A game to teach us how to read.
Mrs. L.:	What does the Cat in the Hat say the trick is to reading words?
Amy:	Twenty-six letters. I know the letters.
Kelly:	I think there are more than twenty-six letters.
Wyatt:	Maybe we should count them.

Mrs. L.:	Maybe there's something in the box to help us with that.
Amy:	I'll check for you. Look, it's a bunch of letters.
Mrs. L.:	Let's put the letters on the board. Gary, would you choose a letter from the bag, please?
Gary:	It's a *J*.
Mrs. L.:	Great! The sound for the letter *J* is . . .
Class:	*J-J-J*.
Mrs. L.:	Nice work. Lucy, please choose another letter.
Lucy:	It's *B*.
Mrs. L.:	The sound for the letter *B* is . . .
Class:	*B-B-B*. *(We continue identifying the letters in the box and their sounds before placing them on the board in scrambled order.)*
Wyatt:	The box is empty.
Kelly:	Did we get them all? We should count them.
Mrs. L.:	Good idea. *(The class counts 26 letters.)*
Mrs. L.:	Let's put the letters in *ABC* order to make sure we didn't miss any. Say the alphabet slowly while I arrange the letters in order from *A* to *Z*. *(The class repeats the alphabet.)* Now let's count the letters again. *(The class counts 26 letters again.)* That means there are twenty-six letters in the whole alphabet. Words are made with letters. Let's try the Cat in the Hat's game. We'll spell a few words and see what happens. First, spell *cat*.
Kyle:	I know how. *C-A-T* spells *cat*. *(Kyle spells the word with the magnetic letters.)*
Mrs. L.:	Great! If we take away the *C*, what is left?
Class:	*A-T*.
Mrs. L.:	Right, *A-T* makes *AT*.
Tyler:	That's a word.
Mrs. L.:	You're right. Tell me how *at* might be used in a sentence.
Brian:	I was at my Grandma's house.
Kevin:	We are at school.
Mrs. L.:	Nice work. Let's put the *H* with *AT*. Now we have . . .
Class:	*HAT*.
Mrs. L.:	Right! Let's try this with other letters. Go to the beginning of the alphabet and put the *B* with *AT*.
Lauren:	That would be *B-AT*. *Bat!*
Mrs. L.:	Right! So far you've read the words *cat*, *hat*, and *bat*. I'll put the letter *B* here with the *C* and the *H* since they all make real words with *AT*. Let's try another letter. *D* is next. *D* with *AT* makes . . .
Marc:	*DAT*. I never heard of that.
Kevin:	You just said it! I never heard of *DAT*.
Mrs. L.:	Actually, *that* is spelled *T-H-A-T*. How do you like that?
Marc:	Not *D-A-T*?
Mrs. L.:	Words are funny. There are so many of them, and many sound very similar. Reading lots of books and listening to lots of stories is the best way I know to

become familiar with lots of different words. Since *D-A-T* is not a word, I'll put the *D* back in the alphabet line. Let's try another letter with *AT*.

Leah: *E* would make *E-AT*.

Mrs. L.: If *E-A-T* were part of the sound-alike word family of *AT* it would be *E-AT*, and that is not a word. But *E-A-T* actually is a word. You use this word every time you eat.

Class: *EAT!*

Joni: Is that how you spell *eat*?

Mrs. L.: Yes. We'll put the letter *E* off to the side since it's a special letter with *AT*. Time to put the next letter with *AT*.

Tara: That's *F* for *F-AT*.

Tyler: I see a fat cat in a hat.

Mrs. L.: Wow! You sure used a lot of *AT* words in that sentence. We'll put *F* with *C, H,* and *B*. What's next?

Paul: *J-AT*.

Mrs. L.: Sometimes *G* makes the *J-J-J* sound. But other times *G* has a hard *G-G-G* sound like in *goat*.

Rebecca: *J-AT* and *G-AT* aren't really words.

Mrs. L.: Then we should put *G* with the *D* to show the letters that don't make words found in books. We already know *H-A-T* makes a word. *I* is a vowel. Vowels make two different sounds—long and short. *I-A-T* would either make the word *I-AT (with a long* i *sound)*, or *I-AT (with a short* i *sound)*.

Kyle: That doesn't make sense. *J* is next.

Lucy: We tried that already when we did *G*. Put *J* with the not-found-in-book letters.

Wyatt: *K* makes *K-AT!*

Lauren: No, *C-A-T* makes *cat*.

Mrs. L.: Since *K* and *C* both make the "cuh" sound, *K* with *AT* would be sound-spelling for *cat*. When you see *cat* in a book, it's spelled *C-A-T*. Let's make some more *A-T* words. *(We continue for the rest of the alphabet.)*

ON ANOTHER DAY

After school that day, I chart the *a-t* lists shown on the next page by writing the beginning letter in red and *—at* in black. The next day, the children and I read our lists of words, which is hung in a prominent place in our classroom. I challenge them to be on the lookout for other *—at* words in books they read independently or hear during read-aloud. We begin another list titled "More *—at* Words from Books." Words with blends such as *chat, brat, drat, scat,* and *flat* top this list.

Real -at words book-spelled		-at words not found in books		Non-rhyming -at words
at	pat	dat	qat	eat
bat	rat	gat	uat	oat
cat	sat	iat	wat	
fat	tat	jat	xat	
hat	vat	kat	yat	
mat		lat	zat	

With the magnetic letters and the note from the Cat in the Hat back in the shoebox and the *a-t* charts hung nearby, a word study center has been created. Students construct and read the *-at* words independently using our lists as a reference. After everyone has had a chance to practice reading the *-at* words at the center, copy the words onto index cards for students to practice reading in isolation.

As individual students are able to read the words on the cards (with assistance), they receive a badge that reads: I Can Read *AT* Words All By Myself! This badge is worn proudly by students who are happy to proclaim their new reading knowledge.

MORE FUN WITH THE BOOK

Have students design a hat for the Cat in the Hat. Set up an art center where they can glue red stripes onto a large white hat outline. To complete the hat, ask students to add a few *AT* family words to the hat using self-stick foam alphabet letters.

Cat in the Hat badge

Teaching With Favorite Read-Alouds in Kindergarten

More Must-Have Books for Reinforcing Reading Readiness Skills

Polar Bear, Polar Bear, What Do You Hear?
by Bill Martin Jr. and John Archambault

 **LEARNING ABOUT** Letter-Sound Relationships

Polar Bear, Polar Bear, what do you hear?
I hear a lion roaring in my ear.
Lion, Lion, what do you hear?
I hear a hippopotamus snorting in my ear . . .
— From *Polar Bear, Polar Bear, What Do You Hear?*, pages 2–5

Apply the rollicking question-and-answer pattern of this book to an oral response letter-sound recognition game. Polar Bear and the sounds his friends make can help students discern the different sounds that letters of the alphabet make. Begin by chanting a student's name and saying, "What do you hear?". Students repeat an animal's name, stressing the beginning letter sound. The whole class responds to the chant.

Mrs. L.:	Marc, Marc, what do you hear?
Marc:	I hear a lion. L-L Lion.
Mrs. L.:	Lion, Lion, what letter makes that sound?
Class:	The letter *L* makes that sound.
Mrs. L.:	Lucy, Lucy, what do you hear?
Lucy:	I hear a cow. C-C Cow.
Mrs. L.:	Cow, Cow, what letter makes that sound?
Class:	The letter *C* makes that sound.

Challenge your students to identify an animal for each consonant letter of the alphabet.

ON ANOTHER DAY
Individual students chant the sounds they hear while the class responds with the letter that begins each sound. Students learn that *H* makes a hissing sound, *M* makes a mooing sound, *R* makes a roaring sound, and so on. Here's an example of how this word-play game, which reinforces listening skills, oral language, and phonemic awareness goes.

Rich Vocabulary

snarled *v.* growling in a mean way, sometimes showing teeth

yelped *v.* gave a short cry

Mrs. L.:	Leah, Leah, what do you hear?
Leah:	I hear a lion r-r-roaring at me.
Mrs. L.:	Roaring, roaring, what letter makes that sound?
Class:	You need an *R* to make a roaring sound.
Mrs. L.:	Gary, Gary, what do you hear?
Gary:	I hear a cow m-m-mooing at me.
Mrs. L.:	Mooing, mooing, what letter makes that sound?
Class:	You need an *M* to make a mooing sound.

MORE FUN WITH THE BOOK

Another fun activity that sharpens listening skills is the game, Zookeeper Says. In this take-off of Simon Says, take the role of the Zookeeper and direct the class to growl like a polar bear, snort like a hippo, hiss like a boa constrictor, and so on—but only when the Zookeeper says.

The Zookeeper says roar like a lion.
Flute like a flamingo.
Bray like a zebra.
The Zookeeper says trumpet like an elephant.
Snarl like a leopard.
The Zookeeper says yelp like a peacock.
Bellow like a walrus.

....

Alphabet Under Construction
by Denise Fleming

 **Letter and Phonemic Awareness**

Mouse airbrushes the A,
buttons the B,
carves the C,
dyes the D,
erases the E . . .
— From *Alphabet Under Construction*, pages 2–7

The memorable and vividly painted pictures (created with pulp painting) are accented with simple text to make this book a perfect resource for reinforcing letter recognition, letter sounds, and using meaning clues to decode unknown words. It gives new meaning to the concept of working with the alphabet.

Read aloud *Alphabet Under Construction* page by page, and watch as students proudly "read" the words using the bold picture and letter-sound clues to decode the one-word descriptions of Mouse's construction of the letters from *A* to *Z*. To reinforce left to right progression, call on students to take turns pointing to each word as it is read. Also discuss how the print is organized on the page with spaces between each word describing Mouse's work.

Share Mouse's tentative and completed work schedules shown on the back of the book and on the last page. Explain your own plan to construct the alphabet in your classroom. Use 9-by-9-inch cutout letters and the ideas on the Alphabet Work Schedule shown here to help students make individual alphabets of their own.

ALPHABET WORK SCHEDULE

Monday	Tuesday	Wednesday	Thursday	Friday
A Airbrush *A* with Blo-Pens.	**B** Glue buttons on *B*.	**C** Cut out a *C* with scissors.	**D** Dip a *D* in dye (water mixed with tempura paint).	**E** Color *E* with chalk, then erase.
F Fold an *F*.	**G** Glue the line on the *G*.	**H** Punch holes in an *H* to hang with string.	**I** Ice an *I* with paint mixed with glue.	**J** Make a ribbon to judge *J*. Glue it on *J*.
K Use two straws to kink the *K*; tape on a cutout *K*.	**L** Draw straight lines on the *L* with markers and a ruler.	**M** Measure an *M*. Make tally marks.	**N** Nail an *N* with paper fasteners.	**O** Okay an *O* by writing *OK* all over it.
P Plant a *P* by putting in it a cutout pot.	**Q** Quilt a *Q* with yarn.	**R** Paint an *R* with little rollers.	**S** Stamp an *S* with rubber stamps.	**T** Tile a *T* with paper tiles.
U Unroll a *U* after rolling it and taping the top to paper.	**V** Velcro a *V* onto violet paper.	**W** Wallpaper a *W* with wallpaper scraps.	**X** X-ray an *X* with chalk on black paper.	**Y** Yank a yellow *Y*. **Z** Make zebra stripes on *Z*.

NOTE: Blo-pens are available at art supply stores. To make zebra stripes, use Miss Christy's trick: Place a white cutout *Z* in a plastic tub. Dip marbles in black paint, place in tub, and roll over the *Z* to make stripes.

Have students glue the completed alphabet letters onto background paper and store them in folders. Staple the completed pages from *A* to *Z* together into a Picture Dictionary of the *Alphabet Under Construction*. Designate wall space to display a sample of the final alphabet.

Lauren's zebra-striped Z

Mouse Mess
by Linnea Riley

LEARNING ABOUT

Beginning Letter Sounds

Rich Vocabulary

scattered *v.* thrown here and there; spread about

This book is a yummy feast for Mouse, a visual treat for students, and a teacher's best book pick for teaching beginning letter sounds. As Mouse dips his toes in raspberry jam, builds castle walls of brown sugar, and rakes and jumps into piles of corn flakes, he makes a mess! Read aloud this rhyming word text, and let students pore over the intricate illustrations. Mouse's cozy bed made from a converted sardine can, the wristwatch clock hanging on the wall, the jingle bell doorbell, and the broom made from a kitchen basting brush are just a few of the illustrations that grab young readers' interest from the very first page.

Challenge students to find an item in Mouse's mess for each letter of the alphabet. Copy each letter at the top of 26 large index cards, and display them on the chalk ledge. As students discover the treats in the mess, write the words on the index cards—*bread* on the *B* card; *crackers, corn flakes,* and *cookies* on the *C* card, and so on. After all the items from *Mouse Mess* have been identified, fill any empty letter cards with students' favorite snacks. Then scramble the cards, and have students "clean up" by placing them in alphabetic order. End the activity by reviewing the letters and words on the cards.

Snacks from *Mouse Mess*	Our Favorite Snacks to Add to *Mouse Mess*
cornflakes, sardines, cookies, Oreos, milk, cheese, apple, oranges, bananas, raspberry jam, peanut butter, bread, brown sugar, olives, catsup, pickles, pretzels, pizza	donuts, enchiladas, French fries, fruit bars, grapes, honey, ice cream, Kix, licorice, nuts, Tootsie rolls, Ugli fruit, valentine candy hearts, watermelon, yogurt, Zagnut bars, popcorn

MORE FUN WITH THE BOOK

Place the *A–Z* word cards at a center stocked with magazines from which students can cut and glue pictures of the snacks to help with word identification. You may also provide a scrap paper box, scissors, and glue so they can explore Linnea Riley's collage technique. After cutting and arranging paper to resemble Oreos, olives, or another snack from the mouse mess, students can glue the collage snacks onto the index cards. For printing and word identification practice, encourage them to dictate or label each snack with sound-spelled words.

O is for Oreos.

....

Eating the Alphabet:
Fruits and Vegetables from A to Z
by Lois Ehlert

LEARNING ABOUT

Identifying Fruits and Vegetables

Apple to Zucchini,
come take a look.
Start eating your way
through this alphabet book.
   — From *Eating the Alphabet: Fruits and Vegetables from A to Z*, page 1

Lois Ehlert's book includes many words less common to a kindergartner's vocabulary—or perhaps less preferred by a kindergartner's taste buds! Although brussels sprouts, asparagus, **and** zucchini are sure to get a few

---

Rich Vocabulary

unfamiliar *adj.* not known

"yuks" during this read-aloud, students can't help but be impressed with Ehlert's creativity in putting together a collection of fruits and vegetables from *A* to *Z*.

After reading aloud the book, send home a request for fruit and vegetable donations for a taste-testing party where students eat an alphabet of their own. Once the fruits and vegetables have been collected, gather the class together to identify and label each donation with its beginning letter. Then arrange the donations in alphabetic order.

Have a parent volunteer on hand to cut the fruits and vegetables into small bites for

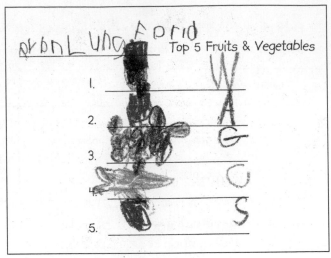

Ryan's Top 5 Fruits and Vegetables

each student to taste. Pass out paper plates, and invite students to taste as many different fruits and vegetables as they desire. Provide a recording sheet for them to draw and write the beginning letters or names of their top five fruits and vegetables.

Alphabears
by Kathleen Hague

LEARNING ABOUT **Letter and Name Recognition**

Alphabears provides a warm and fuzzy way to extend name and alphabet recognition. As each teddy bear is introduced in the book, a name becomes associated with a letter. To your student's delight, there are sure to be a few bear names that match their own.

Prior to the read-aloud, ask students to write their names on precut paper letters that match the beginning letters of their first names. Gather students around you by reciting the alphabet; for example, as *A* is called, Amy and Andrew come to the gathering space with their *A*s, and so on. Display the students' letters under the *Alphabears* set of letters.

Alphabear Names:

Amanda	Byron	Charles	Devon	Elsie	Freddie	Gilbert	Henry
A	*B*	*C*	*D*	*E*	*F*	*G*	*H* . . .

Our Names:

Amy	Brian					Grant
Andrew						Gary

Teaching With Favorite Read-Alouds in Kindergarten

As you read aloud the story, write the names of the alphabears on corresponding blank letters: *Amanda* on the letter *A*, and so on. Pause to make observations such as "David sounds like Devon, which means these names both start with *D*." After all the alphabear names have been recorded, beginning letters identified, and common names highlighted, tally your findings to find the most common beginning letter of the names in the class, the least common, the letter in second place, any ties, and so on.

MORE FUN WITH THE BOOK

- Name sorting is a favorite activity of mine because it helps students look at words in more than one way. Display all the students' names. Choose those with a common attribute such as those with the same number of letters, names that begin or end with the same two letters, and so on. Students must identify the common attribute and then add any other names from the class that belong in a particular group.
- On many pages in the book, the featured letter is illustrated within the context of the picture—*T* for *Tammy* is etched in the details of her chair, *Q* for *Quimbly* appears on his hat, *F* for *Freddie* is monogrammed on his bath towel. Although I was unable to find an illustration to go with every letter, I would challenge you and your students to look closely for yourselves. The illustrations are certainly worth a second examination.

For a related read-aloud, be sure to read *Numbears*, which is also written by Kathleen Hague and illustrated by Michael Hague.

Olivia Saves the Circus
by Ian Falconer

 **LEARNING ABOUT** Sound-Spelling

This sequel to *Olivia* portrays the determined pig with a mind of her own at her best. After cooking breakfast for her "old and new" younger brothers, donning her "boring" uniform and Olivia-izing it, she heads to school. Not surprising, Olivia "always blossoms in front of an audience." So when it's time to tell the class about her vacation, she is more than eager to describe the time she went to the circus and all the circus people had ear infections. But have no fear—as Olivia the Tattooed Lady, Madame Olivia the Dog Trainer, Olivia the Queen of the Trampoline, and others, Olivia saves the circus. Although the teacher has her doubts, Olivia says the story is "pretty all true—to the best of her recollection."

Use the fact that Olivia "knew how to do everything" at the circus to help your students learn everything about sound-spelling. Brainstorm a list of the acts Olivia performed at the circus. As students name each circus act, draw a simple picture for each act on white construction paper—a line for the tight rope, a hoop for the dog trainer, a swing for the Flying Olivia, balls for juggling, and so on. Together, sound-spell the words that describe each act. I encourage and accept one-letter representations for words, labels with illustrations, and main sounds in our sound-spelling efforts. Some examples are shown below.

Circus Acts

Tit rop wokr	dog tranr
lin tamr	qen uv the trampolen
tatood lade	usd stilts
jugld	clwn
rod a unisicl	fliing Olivia

To close the activity, remind students of the following reasons for recording ideas on paper:
1. A writer can read the idea at a later time.
2. Others are able to read the writer's idea without the writer being present.
Explain that when an idea is communicated with letters and pictures, successful writing has been achieved.

....

Sheila Rae, the Brave
by Kevin Henkes

LEARNING ABOUT

How Print Is Organized

Look out, Olivia, here's another spunky female with attitude named Sheila Rae, the Brave. Kevin Henkes, author of the great books *Wemberly Worried, Chrysanthemum, A Weekend with Wendell,* and *Lilly's Purple Plastic Purse,* has created yet another memorable character for children to love. Young readers will be inspired by this confident little mouse who isn't afraid of anything—not the dark, thunder and lightning, or even the big black dog at the end of the block. Who else but Sheila Rae would growl at stray dogs and bare her teeth at stray cats?

Read aloud this book to find out what happens when Sheila Rae's brave nature overcomes common sense and turns the fearless mouse into a helpless, panic-stricken and lost mouse. Then let Sheila Rae's high self-esteem help your students understand how print is organized. Ask students to define what it means to be brave—to be strong when you are really scared. Call on a volunteer to share his or her bravest moment. Write the student's name and the

Teaching With Favorite Read-Alouds in Kindergarten

words *was brave when* at the top of a sheet of chart paper. As the student describes the moment, add a blank for each word to illustrate that print conveys meaning in the form of word units.

Joey was brave when <u>he got a shot</u>.

Explain that each blank is for one word in the idea. Talk students through

the spelling of each word unit as you record it in book-spelling.

Demonstrate a "two-finger space" to separate each word in the idea. Count the number of words in the sentence versus the number of letters in each word to further illustrate how print is organized.

Kick off read-aloud or gathering time each day by assisting one or two more volunteers with their bravest moment chart pages. After everyone has had a chance to dictate a chart page, fasten the pages together and attach a cover to fashion a class big book based on *Sheila Rae, the Brave*.

Working on a page for our class big book

The Cookie-Store Cat
by Cynthia Rylant

LEARNING ABOUT **Organizing Letters and Words**

Use Cynthia Rylant's kid-friendly, childlike illustrations to give students a chance to explore art, cookie decorating, and organizing letters in words and words in sentences—all in one lesson. Read aloud the book to discover how this lucky feline came to be the cookie-store cat who is "sweeter than any cookie the bakers have ever baked, prettier than marzipan and a real gumdrop gem."

Following the read-aloud, display a magnetic chalkboard as your "cookie sheet." Place magnetic letters from the words in *I like the cookie-store cat* in scrambled order across the top of the chalkboard (for example, *I keli eth cookie tsoer act*). Also write the sentence on a large sheet of chart paper. Ask students to refer to the chart paper sentence to help you arrange the words in book-spelled order.

Next provide your students with paper, markers, scissors, and cookie cutters to trace, cut out, and decorate cookie-store cats, gingerbread men, Santa Claus faces and other shapes inspired by the book. After students have glued the cookies onto black paper "cookie sheets," pass out snack bags with the words from the book title on separate strips of paper. You can also include picture clues for the nouns.

Tell students to place the words in order at the top of the black paper before decorating their cookie creations with "icing" (3D washable paint pens) or colored chalk for labeling.

A cookie sheet

ON ANOTHER DAY

- Choose a few different cookies to feature in a class graph. Have children attach self-stick notes on the graph to show which cookie they like best.
- For an added treat, use one of the recipes on the last two pages of the book for a fun book-based cooking lesson. Pass out Cinnamon Sugarplums or Gumdrop Gems to the helpers in your school—after students taste-test the cookies, of course!
- Be sure to share *The Bookshop Dog* by Cynthia Rylant (Blue Sky Press, 1996). Young readers enjoy the fact that the cookie-store cat is a neighbor of Martha Jane, the bookshop-dog. This canine and her friends make an appearance in *The Cookie-Store Cat*.

....

Top Cat
by Lois Ehlert

LEARNING ABOUT **Rhyming Words**

For more feline reading, follow your book celebration of *The Cookie-Store Cat* with a little *Top Cat* fun. The collage-cut illustrations together with the text's rollicking rhyming beat make this book a kindergarten favorite for reading again and again.

Read aloud what happens when a new cat invades Top Cat's territory. After your initial read-aloud and discussion, read the story several more times. Talk about how rhyming words sound alike, but they may not always be spelled alike.

Rich Vocabulary

dull *adj.* not any fun

invaded *v.* attacked

Teaching With Favorite Read-Alouds in Kindergarten

Prior to the lesson, chart parts of the story, deleting the second rhyming word in each pair.

> *Boring job! Never see a mouse.*
> *Nothing much happens in this dull _____.*

Keep little fingers on task during the activity by providing lapboards, paper, pencils, and cat-shaped paper that you've cut out earlier. Talk students through the process of how rhyming words work: *If m-m-m-ouse is spelled M-O-U-S-E, then h-h-h-ouse must be spelled H-O-U-S-E. The M changes to H, but the O-U-S-E stays the same.* As you write the missing rhyming words on the chart, students should copy the words onto their cat-shaped paper.

(See *100 Skill-Building Lessons Using 10 Favorite Books* by Susan Lunsford [Scholastic Professional Books, 2001] for art projects, word study, and writing and math activities based on Lois Ehlert's *Top Cat*.)

Top Cat rhyming words

Even More Must-Have Books for Reading Readiness Skills

Clifford the Big Red Dog by Norman Bridwell

In the Small, Small Pond by Denise Fleming

Miss Bindergarten Gets Ready for Kindergarten by Joseph Slate

Mooncake by Frank Asch

Animalia by Graeme Base

Night Noises by Mem Fox

Curious George Learns the Alphabet by H.A. Rey

Does a Kangaroo Have a Mother, Too? by Eric Carle

Little Rabbit's First Word Book by Alan Baker

Nuts to You by Lois Ehlert

Lyle, Lyle, Crocodile by Bernard Waber

Green Eggs and Ham by Dr. Seuss

Somebody and the Three Blairs by Marilyn Tolhurst

Chapter 2: Sing Along with Me!
10 Must-Have Books of
Read-Along Songs and Rhymes

Chapter Learning Goals:
* building fluency with repeated readings of familiar verses, songs, and poems
* reading with expression
* making simple inferences regarding the order of events and possible outcomes of a story
* discussing setting, main characters, main events, sequence, and problems in stories
* relating stories to personal experiences
* stimulating oral language development
* understanding level-appropriate sight words and vocabulary
* enjoying great rhyming, sing-along books

Classic songs and memorable rhymes from authors and illustrators such as Iza Trapani, Nadine Bernard Westcott, Mary Ann Hoberman, and Bruce Whatley get a new twist in this chapter. Build kindergartners' confidence by giving them the opportunity to "read" aloud familiar songs and rhymes as well as new verses with fluency and expression.

Read Mary Ann Hoberman's version of *The Eensy-Weensy Spider*, and then order the events that happened the day she went up the waterspout. Reinforce fluency and the patterns of rhymes with *Over in the Meadow*. Use Iza Trapani's continuation of *Twinkle, Twinkle, Little Star* to reinforce word identification. Sequence events, make predictions, and then retell Will Hillenbrand's version of *Down by the Station*. Take a bus ride, and read along as the *Wheels On the Bus* go 'round and 'round. Make puppets to frolic along with *Five Little Monkeys Jumping on the Bed*. Join Steven Kellogg's nicknack paddywhack band in *Give the Dog a Bone*. Learn to read the days of the week with Eric Carle's *Today Is Monday*. Solve Tiny Tim's problem with the help of *The Lady with the Alligator Purse*, and celebrate *The Teddy Bears' Picnic* by sequencing and recording the events of the day. Get students ready to read aloud, talk and write about, and sing along with the ten must-have books in this chapter!

---

10 Must-Have Books of
Read-Along Songs and Rhymes

The Eensy-Weensy Spider by Mary Ann Hoberman

Over in the Meadow by Jane Cabrera

Twinkle, Twinkle, Little Star by Iza Trapani

Down by the Station by Will Hillenbrand

Wheels on the Bus by Raffi

Five Little Monkeys Jumping on the Bed by Eileen Christelow

Give the Dog a Bone by Steven Kellogg

Today Is Monday by Eric Carle

The Lady with the Alligator Purse by Nadine Bernard Westcott

The Teddy Bears' Picnic by Jerry Garcia

The Eensy-Weensy Spider
by Mary Ann Hoberman

LEARNING ABOUT Sequencing

The eensy-weensy spider went up the waterspout.
Down came the rain and washed the spider out.
Out came the sun and dried up all the rain.
And the eensy-weensy spider went up the spout again.
— From *The Eensy-Weensy Spider*, page 3

Rich Vocabulary

brook *n.* a creek

Not many children make it to kindergarten without knowing about the eensy-weensy spider. In Mary Ann Hoberman's adaptation of this classic sing-along rhyme, the eensy-weensy spider went up the waterspout again. She sings, swims, joins a parade, and goes shopping for shoes, among other antics. Share this story with your class, and on the next day, lead your students in a lesson on sequencing the events of the story and stimulating oral language development.

When students arrive on the morning of this mini-lesson, have copies of page 39 available for them to color and cut into story cards. Enlarge a copy of the reproducible for demonstration purposes as well. Draw a large spider web outline with 12 sections like the one shown on page 40, settle students around you with their completed story cards, and launch a lesson that orders the events of the eensy-weensy spider's day from beginning to end.

Mrs. L.: Yesterday, we read *The Eensy-Weensy Spider* for read-aloud. This morning, you made story cards with words and pictures to represent different events from the story. I have a copy of those same cards with me, but my cards are all mixed up. Let's reread the story, and put the cards in order on this big spider web.

Kyle:	Then the eensy-weensy spider will always remember her day.
Mrs. L.:	Exactly. And you'll be able to retell her story. We all know what happened first: "The eensy-weensy spider"—
Class:	—"went up the waterspout."
Mrs. L.:	Right! Which story card represents this first event in her day?
Jordan:	The waterspout with the letters *U-P*.
Marc:	*U-P* is *up*.
Mrs. L.:	Right! She went up the waterspout. Marc, please put this story card on the first section of the web. Let's read this page together, and make hand motions as she walks up the waterspout. *(The students echo the words and make hand motions as I read.)* Now let's look at the next page.

Sequencing *The Eensy-Weensy Spider*

Rebecca:	It's the one where she's singing. The word is *LA*. Like "la-la-la-la."
Mrs. L.:	Great reading! Please be my echo again. *(The students echo the words and make hand motions as I read.)*
Rebecca:	I'll put the word *LA* on the web beside the waterspout.
Mrs. L.:	Thank you. Let's keep reading.
Tara:	This is the page where she hugs the baby bug too tight.
Kelly:	And the mom-bug gets mad.
Mrs. L.:	Let's read it together. *(The children repeat the page line by line as above.)*
Mrs. L.:	You'll have to do some reading to find the story card that goes with this page.
Leah:	The words aren't in the picture like the word *LA*.
Mrs. L.:	Right. But you just said both the words when you were my echo.
Kevin:	Is it the *U-G-H* card?
Mrs. L.:	Maybe . . . What do you think *U-G-H* spells?
Kevin:	*Hug*!
Mrs. L.:	*Hug* starts with *H-H-H*. The first word on the card has the same letters as *hug*, but they're in a different order. It begins with the *U-U-U* sound as in *UP*, and it rhymes with *hug*.
Kevin:	The word is *ugh*!
Tyler:	*Ugh* and *hug*.
Mrs. L.:	What great word detectives you are. Let's put these words on our web.
Grant:	Turn the page. I think the one where she falls in the lake is next.
Renee:	No, look, she gets caught in the rain.
Gary:	But the sun dries her out like chalk.
Mrs. L.:	Excellent remembering. Let's see if we can find a card that goes with the picture on this page.
Brian:	It's the one with the worm on an apple or tomato. I'm not sure what those words are.

Teaching With Favorite Read-Alouds in Kindergarten

Mrs. L.:	Let's read the words on the page and listen for a word that starts with *G* and one that starts with *P*. These are the beginning letter clues on the story card with the tomato. "The eensy-weensy spider walked down the garden path"—
Joni:	That's it! The words are *garden path*! I knew it.
Mrs. L.:	Great listening. Get your fingers ready. We'll have her walk down the garden path while you be my echo.
Gary:	We'll have to get the sun out, too, because that's what dries her up like chalk.
Mrs. L.:	Okay. Here we go. *(Students echo the words and make hand motions as I read.)*
Mrs. L.:	Any guesses about what the spider does next?
Kelly:	Marches in the band.
Kyle:	Swims with the frog.
Mrs. L.:	I'll turn the page, and we'll see.
Kyle:	I was right! The frog's telling her to get *O-U-T*. I see that word on the story card. Does *O-U-T* spell *out*?
Mrs. L.:	Yes, it does. Let's read the page together—and get your *S* swimming arms out.
Amy:	And your finger to point OUT like the frog is doing.
Mrs. L.:	Excellent idea. *(The students echo the words and make hand motions as I read.)*
Mrs. L.:	It looks like we're halfway through the spider's day. So far she's gone up the waterspout, sung *la*, hugged a bug, walked down the garden path, and swam with a frog. Look at the story cards that are left, and predict what happens next.
Wyatt:	She eats her soup and goes to sleep at the very end.
Mrs. L.:	I agree. What does she do before she eats her soup?
Wyatt:	She has to get home, and it's dark so the glowworm helps her.
Mrs. L.:	Excellent remembering.
Rebecca:	Before that she buys shoes and then scrapes her knees.
Mrs. L.:	Let's keep reading. You've almost filled up the entire web. *(We continue reading, making hand motions, and adding story cards to our eensy-weensy spider web. Our lesson ends with the realization that this story could continue indefinitely.)*
Marc:	When the eensy-weensy spider wakes up, she'll probably go up the spout again!
Grant:	Then the story will start all over again!
Kevin:	Or, maybe something else will happen.
Kelly:	Maybe she looks at a book.
Lauren:	Or takes a bath.
Tyler:	Or brushes her teeth. Every day something else might happen.

When students return to their seats, hand out copies of the reproducible on page 40 and let them arrange their story cards in order on their webs. They can use their webs and cards to tell and retell *The Eensy-Weensy Spider* at home.

On another day, we place our large spider web on the floor and make a spinner by putting a paper clip in the center of the web and placing the tip of a pencil inside the clip. Students spin the paper clip with the flick of their fingers. When the paper clip lands on a section, we practice reading the corresponding page with hand motions. The children, now very familiar with the book, fill in the rhyming words orally.

More Must-Have Books of Read-Aloud Songs and Rhymes

....

Over in the Meadow
by Jane Cabrera

LEARNING ABOUT **Enhancing Fluency**

Over in the meadow in the sand in the sun
lived Old Mother Turtle and her little turtle one.
"Dig," said the mother. "I dig," said the one.
So they dug all day in the sand in the sun.
— From *Over in the Meadow*, page 2

This classic children's song gets a redo in Jane Cabrera's colorful book. Teach the song, read the book, and reread it for a book-based lesson on rhyming word patterns to enhance fluency. As illustrated above with the words *sun, one, one, sun*, this A-B-B-A pattern continues throughout the book as other little animals obey their mothers' orders to bask, wiggle, twitch, tuwhoo, and more over in the meadow. Incidental reinforcement of the words *over, in, the, meadow, all, day, old, mother, and,* and *said* occurs through their repetitive use on each page as well.

Copy the following lines onto sentence strips, and attach magnetic stick-strips to the back of each strip. Have blank sentence strips available for filling in the words that change for each different animal page from one to ten. You may wish to copy the number words onto index cards ahead of time to allow children to choose the appropriate word and numeral for each animal rhyme.

Over in the meadow _____
lived Old Mother _____ and her little _____.
"_____," said the mother. "We _____," said
the _____.
So they _____ all day _____.

As a group, reread *Over in the Meadow*. Pause to fill in the missing words for each different page of animals. Take advantage of this opportunity to demonstrate book-spelling for the missing words. To reinforce word recognition, reread the completed rhymes and point

> ## Rich Vocabulary
>
> **meadow** *n.* an open field of grass
>
> **gnaw** *v.* to chew

out each word as students read along. Provide a copy of the reproducible on page 41 for each student to complete and read with a friend.

MORE FUN WITH THE BOOK

Got a few spare minutes? Have students dictate a new favorite animal rhyme. Identify an animal word, and then think of a number word with a rhyming word where the animal can be over in the meadow. The words *cat, two* and *in a shoe* work for the rhyme below.

> Over in the meadow <u>inside an old shoe</u>
> lived Old Mother <u>Cat</u> and her little <u>kittens two</u>.
> "<u>Mew</u>," said the mother. "We <u>mew</u>," said the <u>two</u>.
> So they <u>mewed</u> all day <u>inside an old shoe</u>.

....

Twinkle, Twinkle, Little Star
by Iza Trapani

 **LEARNING ABOUT** ## Word Identification

Twinkle, twinkle, star so bright,
Winking at me in the night.
How I wish that I could fly,
And visit you up in the sky.
I wish I may, I wish I might,
Have the wish I wish tonight.

— From *Twinkle, Twinkle, Little Star,* page 4

In Iza Trapani's lovely and expanded retelling of this childhood favorite, the little girl's wish comes true. Together, the girl and the star take a journey into the night, providing a warm reassurance that while the world sleeps, the little star will "twinkle bright on everyone who needs my light": from shedding light on ships lost at sea, on cities, farms, babies held in loving arms, puppies, ponies, birds in trees, to "sleepy children—just like me."

Share this beautiful adaptation of the classic rhyme and then reinforce word identification and fluency with this book-based activity. Chart the familiar verses from "Twinkle, Twinkle, Little Star," and make a copy of the verses for each student. Have students cut out and arrange the lines to the song in order. After reading the lines to you so you can check the order, students may glue the sentence strips onto sky blue construction paper. Provide time for decorating the completed rhyme with foil star stickers or construction-paper stars. Send the rhymes home for more reading and singing fun.

> **Rich Vocabulary**
> **soar** *v.* to fly

ON ANOTHER DAY

Set up a center where each child can draw a star using the steps below and then make a wish. Instruct students to write their wishes using sound-spelling and glitter glue. Hang their stars from the ceiling.

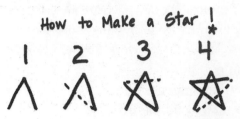

> ## TEACHING TIP
>
> ### A Poem of the Week
>
> Kick off gathering time each day by selecting a child to lead the class in a reading of a favorite charted poem. The leader's tasks include pointing to each word in the poem as the rest of the class reads along, highlighting words from the poem for the class to read in isolation, and selecting a new leader for the following day.
>
> "Twinkle, Twinkle, Little Star" is great to use for introducing Poem of the Week because of its familiarity. After choosing a poem, think of an icon to use with it, such as a star for "Twinkle, Twinkle, Little Star" or a cookie for a poem about cookies. Have each student trace the icon, cut it out, and write his or her name on it. Collect the paper icons, and place them in an envelope in your gathering space. Glue these paper shapes onto a chart to signify a student's stint as leader for a particular poem. Attach a corresponding shape to a wooden dowel so each leader has a pointer that reflects the theme of the poem.

Down by the Station
by Will Hillenbrand

 **LEARNING ABOUT**   **Sequencing Events**

Down by the station early in the morning,
See the little puffer-bellies all in a row.
See the engine driver pull his little lever . . .
Puff, puff,
Toot, toot,
Off we go!
  — From *Down by the Station*, pages 5–9

Rich Vocabulary

exit *v.* to leave

Teaching With Favorite Read-Alouds in Kindergarten

Readers can predict the next animal to join the train by finding hints in the illustrations about where the train is heading. These hints as well as the predictable word pattern make this book a perfect pick for an activity on sequencing. To help students retell the story, copy the animal names, baby animal names, and the sounds they make onto sentence strips. Place the strips in scrambled order on a chart.

Explain that six animals in all join the train. Together, reread the story, inviting students to place the animal names, baby animal names, sounds, and collective expressions in order as shown below.

Animal	Baby	Sound
elephant	calf	thrump, thrump
flamingo	chick	peep, peep
panda	cub	grump, grump
tiger	cub	mew, mew
seal	pup	flip, flop
	Uh-oh!	
	Phew!	
kangaroo	joey	bump, bump
	Off we go!	

During independent work time, students may draw or cut out animal pictures from magazines to place beside each animal word. Kick off gathering time by selecting a different individual to lead the class in retelling a page from the story. Have the leader choose his or her favorite animal from the train.

Wheels on the Bus
by Raffi

As students enjoy this rhyming sing-along book, they are being exposed to level-appropriate sight words and vocabulary while reading with fluency and expression.

After teaching the song orally, I introduce this book that portrays a town bus ride "all around the town." Prior to the read-aloud, I arrange student chairs to simulate a bus (two rows of two chairs with an aisle down the middle). Next, I copy the words to the hand motions on 8-inch by 10-inch sheets of construction paper with simple illustrations and place them in order on the chalk ledge.

I put on a hat labeled with the word *driver*, grab a toy steering

> **Rich Vocabulary**
>
> **swish** *v.* to move with a slapping sound

wheel, and invite students to sit on the bus with me. I read the story while they make the hand motions to go with the text. After a few successive readings, I pass the hat and steering wheel to a student. As the new driver takes us around town, I walk around the bus, pointing to each word on the hand-motion cards. When students see the words *swish, swish, swish*, for example, the driver pretends to flick a switch on the bus dashboard and the class makes wind-shield wipers with their hands as we all sing that verse of the song.

Five Little Monkeys Jumping on the Bed
by Eileen Christelow

LEARNING ABOUT Strengthening Oral Language

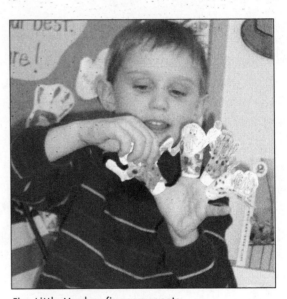
Five Little Monkey finger puppets

After a presumably long day with her five little monkeys, Mama is most likely ready for bed herself. But her little monkeys have other plans that involve jumping on the bed and bumps on heads. The exasperated mother makes five different phone calls to an increasingly irritated doctor. Sense of humor finally restored, Mama ensures that her five little monkeys have fallen fast asleep before having a few good jumps on her own bed!

Your little "monkeys" will enjoy the swinging beat of this predictable story rhyme and the fact that they can read the book all by themselves after a few readings together. Share the book for read-aloud, inviting children to chime in rhyming words and other parts throughout. Once the rhyme is familiar, add finger puppets for additional retellings that will encourage oral language development, fluency, and reading with expression.

Make a copy of the puppets reproducible on page 42 for each student. Have students use colored pencils or crayons to color the five little monkeys. Then they can cut out the puppets and secure them with tape around their fingers. Gather students and their finger puppets. As you read the book, let children act out the monkeys jumping, then remove a monkey each time one "falls off and bumps his head" until all five monkeys are bandaged, ice-packed, and fast asleep.

Rich Vocabulary

rambunctious *adj.*
wild

ON ANOTHER DAY

Copy the number words from *one* to *five* onto index cards. Display the cards as each word appears in the story. After repeated practice, show a word card and ask students to read the word and hold that number of finger puppets. Learning to read number words is more meaningful with the help of the five little monkeys.

More Five Little Monkey Adventures by Eileen Christelow

Five Little Monkeys Sitting in the Tree

Five Little Monkeys Wash the Car

Don't Wake Up Mama

Five Little Monkeys with Nothing to Do

Give the Dog a Bone
by Steven Kellogg

LEARNING ABOUT

Word Recognition

As Steven Kellogg writes in a note at the end of this book: *"This Old Man" is a popular nonsense counting song of uncertain origin ... that seems to have first appeared in the early twentieth century. Hundreds of variations can be found, since improvisation is often the most entertaining part of any singing game; this version takes off in an entirely original direction after the first verse. . . . . It teaches language, counting, rhythm, and coordination.*

Rich Vocabulary

hauled *v.* dragged

The first time I read this book, I was overwhelmed—in a good way! As with any Steven Kellogg book, there is a lot happening in the illustrations. To allow your students the opportunity to hear the flow of the story and the rhythm of the words, I suggest reading or singing the words to the song alone first, inviting them to take in the illustrations privately. Share the book a second time, reading the words in the conversation bubbles along with the text.

Kellogg's retelling of a traditional song from a non-traditional perspective provides wonderful opportunities for oral language development, identifying rhyming word pairs, counting syllables, and more. To reinforce word recognition, copy the number words from *one* to *ten* onto index cards (cut into bone shapes, if you desire). Include separate cards for the words shown beside each number. Display all the cards at the gathering space.

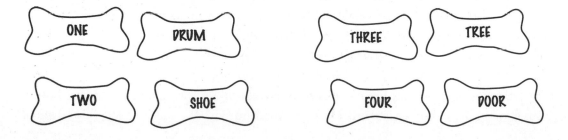

Reread the book, pausing to match each number word to the corresponding item in the story. Provide bone-shaped paper on which students can practice writing the words while a volunteer uses "sticky tack" to place the word pairs together on the board. Discuss strategies for using beginning letter clues and finding similar word chunks to help identify new words (as in *ten* and *hen*). Talk about how all the words pairs are true rhymes except for *one* and *drum*. After the lesson, keep the cards handy so pairs of children can match them during free time.

MORE FUN WITH THE BOOK

Put together a nick-nack paddywhack band that lets students play with the beat of this book. Encourage them to use one or more of the ideas below to create various rhythm instruments. This Nick-Nack Paddywack band can assemble for fun-filled rereadings of Steven Kellogg's hilarious take on "This Old Man."

Nick-Nack Paddywack Instrument Ideas

- empty oatmeal containers decorated and filled with beans for shakers or tapped with spoons like drums
- large dog bones tapped together like rhythm sticks
- paper towel and tissue paper tubes tapped on shoes
- soccer balls tapped with hands like a drum
- toy rhythm instruments brought from home

··

Today Is Monday
by Eric Carle

 **Identifying Days of the Week**

Eric Carle's books provide children with inspiring collage illustrations that invite imitation, simple text that does not intimidate young readers, and fun book-related learning. *Today Is Monday* is no exception, and it makes a perfect springboard for a lesson on saying, reading, and ordering the days of the week, as well as using meaning and structural clues to decode unknown words.

After the initial read-aloud, copy the days of the week onto sentence strips. Have students identify the three letters that are the same in each word: *D-A-Y*. Place a box around these letters in each word, and then use beginning letter clues and other letter-sound clues for help in placing the words in order from *Monday* to *Sunday*. Encourage your students to use the book as a reference.

Next scramble the days of the week strips, and ask a child to pick one. We place the days of the week in order, beginning with the chosen day; if a student chooses Thursday, for example, our list would begin with Thursday and end with Wednesday. With the days of the week fresh in our minds, we have a discussion based on their sequence—"If today is Monday, Friday was three days ago. In three more days it will be Thursday."

ON ANOTHER DAY

I make sentence strips for the food words from the story, and we arrange these words beside the appropriate days of the week. As I reread the story, I invite students to use picture clues from each animal to decode the food word for each day.

Sunday: ice cream   *Saturday: chicken*   *Friday: fresh fish*
Thursday: roast beef   *Wednesday: ZOOOOP*   *Tuesday: spaghetti*
Monday: string beans

Then put picture and structural clues to the test by listing the names of the animals in the book. Have students apply beginning letter and other sound clues to decode the animal words. *NOTE:* If you wish to have students sing the song, the music and words appear at the back of the book. If you are unfamiliar with the tune, ask your music teacher for help, plunk the tune on a piano, or do what I did and make up a tune of your own! As you sing the song, flip backward through the book, using the pictures for clues to each upcoming verse.

....

The Lady with the Alligator Purse
by Nadine Bernard Westcott

LEARNING ABOUT

Building Sight Word Vocabulary

Miss Lucy had a baby,
His name was Tiny Tim,
She put him in the bathtub
To see if he could swim.
He drank up all the water,
He ate up all the soap,
He tried to eat the bathtub,
But it wouldn't go down his throat . . .
 — From *The Lady with the Alligator Purse*, pages 2-8

Nadine Bernard Westcott has once again created a zany surprise ending to another favorite read-along song. While the doctor and nurse believe penicillin and castor oil are the answers to Tiny Tim's "eating disorder," the lady with the alligator purse pulls several boxes of take-out pizza from her purse. As Miss Lucy, Tiny Tim, and the rest of the characters devour their pizza, children will devour the words to this delightfully humorous book.

Read the story again and again, teach the tune, perhaps throw a pizza party, and then make alligator purses. Use lunch-sized paper bags or plain gift bags and the patterns on page 43. After students color and cut out the purse parts, tell them to glue the parts on the paper bag. Show them how to attach lengths of yarn for handles.

Turn the alligator purses into handy storage for sight word practice. Identify three to five simple words from the story for your students to commit to memory: *the, with,* and *see* are words I like to use. Print a set of the words on index cards for each student.

Using our alligator purses

Invite students to meet you on the carpet with their alligator purses. Place a set of word cards in your own alligator purse. Call on individuals to pull the words from your purse, one at a time. Identify the word, and then pass out the corresponding word cards to students to place in their purses. Ask them to recall how the word might have been used by Nadine Bernard Westcott to tell the story.

As the year progresses, these alligator purses become filled with all the new words that students have memorized and learned. They make great reference for use during independent reading and sound-spelling work.

MORE FUN WITH THE BOOK

The possibilities for games to play and learning goals to reinforce with alligator purses are endless.

- Place several stacks of alphabet cards inside a purse, and have students play a version of Go Fish.
- Play a sensory game by placing tactile alphabet cards inside the purse for students to feel and identify.
- Copy rhyming word pairs onto separate index cards. After you place them inside a purse, let students shake it, remove the cards, and match the rhyming pairs.
- Toss a set of alphabet cards into a purse, and shake them up. Set a timer, and then challenge students to arrange the letters in alphabetic order.
- Fill your alligator purse with sight words from the story. Meet one-on-one with students to assess their individual sight word vocabularies.
- Pull alphabet cards from your purse, and call on individuals to identify letters or letter sounds as you display the cards.

The Teddy Bears' Picnic

by Jerry Garcia

LEARNING ABOUT **Sequencing Events**

Beneath the trees, where nobody sees
They'll hide and seek as long as they please
'Cause that's the way the teddy bears
Have their picnic.

— From *The Teddy Bears' Picnic*, pages 14–16

Jerry Garcia and Bruce Whatley have created a bold and impressive picture book version of this classic song that was originally copyrighted by Jimmy Kennedy and John Bratton in 1947. The irresistible bears enjoying a teddy bear picnic give young readers a warm and fuzzy feeling. After sharing this book for read-aloud, I send home a copy of this note with students:

> *Announcing the Annual Teddy Bear Picnic!*
> *Date: February 10*
> *Place: Room 4*
> *Please bring a stuffed bear friend to school to share this celebration with you.*

Rich Vocabulary

disguise *v.* to wear a mask to hide your real appearance

On the day of our Teddy Bear Picnic, the students arrive to find a few of my own bears settled in for a day at school. Several are sitting at a table reading a basket of teddy bear books, one is making a pattern with pattern blocks, another is practicing the alphabet on a mini-sized chalkboard, while a few more are coloring pictures at the art center. And one small, mischievous bear is sitting in the time-out chair.

After greeting each teddy bear with a shake of its paw, I ask owners to make a nametag for his or her bear friend by sound-spelling its name onto a bear-shaped cutout with string attached to it. The students and their bear friends meet

Teddy bears enjoy a special day at school.

with me on the carpet, and we begin our Teddy Bear Picnic. After introductions are made, we arrange the bears in order from smallest to largest in the front row for a rereading of *The Teddy Bear's Picnic.*

As our day progresses, our teddy bears are included in our activities. We end our day with a language experience story that highlights our activities. While students enjoy a snack, I record the highlights of our day as students dictate them to me.

> *Our Teddy Bear's Picnic*
> *Today we had a Teddy Bear picnic. We all brought teddy bears to school. First we introduced our bears to the class. We listened to the story* The Teddy Bears' Picnic. *We drew pictures of our bears. Leah's bear didn't feel well and had to visit the nurse. . . .*

MORE FUN WITH THE BOOK

Math: Count to 20 or higher using teddy bear counters, gummy bears, or teddy-bear shaped cookies. Sort cookies into piles of bears with arms up and bears with arms down; sort counters into groups according to color.

Art: Have students place their teddy bears on paper, trace, cut out, and decorate to look like their special bears.

Writing: Dictate or sound-spell words to finish one of the following sentences:

> If my bear could talk he would tell me _____.
>
> My bear likes to eat _____.
>
> My bear likes to play _____.

Music: Find a recording of *The Teddy Bears' Picnic* to share. Gather students around the book for a sing-along. Point to words as they sing.

Snack Time: End the day with students and bears gathered on a large blanket for a snack of cookies and milk. Reward bears and owners with bear stickers for a great day at school!

Book-Browsing Time: Fill a basket with bear books for students to "read" with bear friends.

Even More Must-Have Books of Read-Along Songs and Rhymes

The Itsy Bitsy Spider retold by Iza Trapani

The Itsy Bitsy Spider by Rosemary Wells

Going to the Zoo by Tom Paxton

I've Been Working on the Railroad illustrated by Nadine Bernard Westcott

Peanut Butter and Jelly: A Play Rhyme illustrated by Nadine Bernard Westcott

Skip to My Lou illustrated by Nadine Bernard Westcott

There Were Ten in the Bed by Pam Adams

Little White Duck by Walt Whippo

Teaching With Favorite Read-Alouds in Kindergarten

Spider Story Cards

Teaching With Favorite Read-Alouds in Kindergarten

Use with *The Eensy-Weensy Spider* adapted by Mary Ann Hoberman.

Teaching With Favorite Read-Alouds in Kindergarten

Use with *The Eensy-Weensy Spider* adapted by Mary Ann Hoberman.

Name _____ Date _____

The Animals Over in the Meadow

Directions: Fill in the blanks.

Over in the meadow in the _____

lived Old Mother _____ and her little _____.

"_____," said the mother.

"We _____," said the _____.

So they _____ all day _____

_____.

Directions: Draw a picture of the animals over in the meadow.

Use with *Over in the Meadow* by Jane Cabrera.

Teaching With Favorite Read-Alouds in Kindergarten

Finger Puppets

Directions:
1. Color the five monkeys. Cut them out.
2. Tape the puppets around your five fingers.

Use with Five Little Monkeys Jumping on the Bed by Eileen Christelow.

Teaching With Favorite Read-Alouds in Kindergarten

Alligator Purse

Directions:
1. Color and cut out the alligator purse parts.
2. Glue the parts onto a paper bag.
3. Tape yarn handles to your alligator purse.

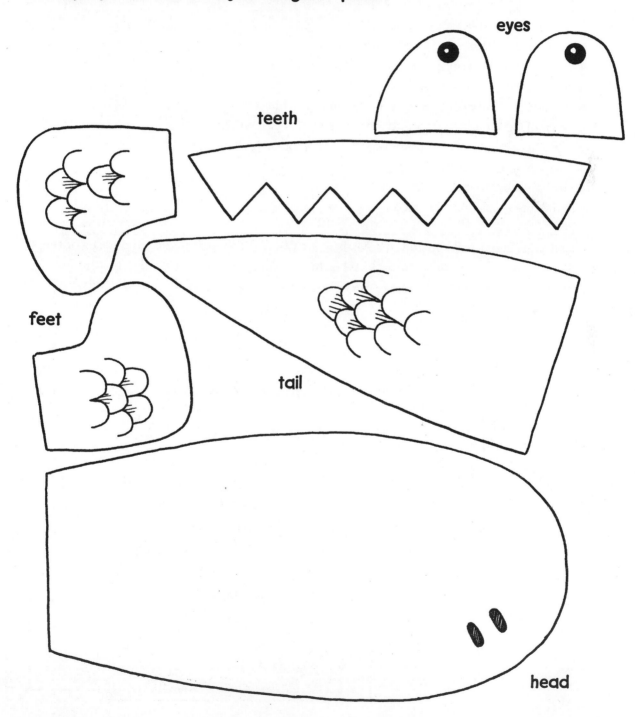

Use with *The Lady with the Alligator Purse* adapted and illustrated by Nadine Bernard Westcott.

Chapter 3: Books to Count on
10 Must-Have Books for Teaching "Math Their Way"

Chapter Learning Goals:

* developing number sense
* identifying and printing numbers from 1 to 100
* estimating number of objects
* using manipulatives to count from 1 to 100
* identifying and continuing 2- and 3-step patterns
* reciting the 12 months of the year
* using manipulatives to count money in a real-life setting
* measuring length using nonstandard units of measurement
* adding and subtracting using objects as manipulatives
* exploring equal parts
* using problem-solving strategies
* enjoying great number books

Several years ago, I participated in a Math Their Way workshop. Based on the ideals of the late Mary Baratta-Lorton, this approach to teaching math is appropriately titled for the way concepts are most effectively taught to very young children: Through the use of hands-on manipulatives, activities that simulate play, and by performing meaningful tasks that relate to jobs in the real world, students do reach learning goals their way. My book-based classroom has grown to include these great books for helping children learn math their way.

Give students *Bunny Money* to go shopping with Max and Ruby. Learn how sipping *Chicken Soup with Rice* is nice all 12 months of the year. Get set for a year of calendar activities with *Miss Bindergarten Celebrates the 100th Day of Kindergarten*. Count on *12 Ways to Get to 11* for developing number sense. Share equal parts with *One of Each*. Explore estimation, addition, and subtraction with *Blueberries for Sal* and measurement with *Inch by Inch*. Ask 20 questions to solve *The Missing Mitten Mystery*. Match patterns in *A Pair of Socks*, and create them with inspiration from *Katy and the Big Snow*.

10 Must-Have Books to Count on

Bunny Money by Rosemary Wells

Chicken Soup with Rice by Maurice Sendak

Miss Bindergarten Celebrates the 100th Day of Kindergarten by Joseph Slate

12 Ways to Get to 11 by Eve Merriam

One of Each by Mary Ann Hoberman

Blueberries for Sal by Robert McCloskey

The Missing Mitten Mystery by Steven Kellogg

Inch by Inch by Leo Lionni

A Pair of Socks by Stuart J. Murphy

Katy and the Big Snow by Virginia Lee Burton

Bunny Money
by Rosemary Wells

 **LEARNING ABOUT** Counting Money

Max's sister, Ruby, saved up a walletful of money for Grandma's birthday present.
"We're going to buy Grandma a music box with skating ballerinas, Max," said Ruby. "Get your lucky quarter and let's go shopping!"

— From *Bunny Money*, pages 2–4

Rich Vocabulary

oozing *v.* dripping

Unfortunately for Max and Ruby, the money runs through their fingers like water. With Max in charge of their last dollar, things don't quite go as planned: Grandma ultimately ends up with a lovely pair of singing bluebird earrings and glow-in-the-dark vampire teeth. Your students are sure to enjoy this funny story featuring this favorite sibling duo. *Bunny Money* provides many different practical math extension ideas such as adding on, subtracting, and counting, all in the context of a great book.

But first, let your students go shopping with Max and Ruby. Prior to the lesson, have a parent volunteer make Bunny Money as shown in the directions for Making Money on the last page of the book. Print enough Bunny Money so each student has one five-dollar bill and ten one-dollar bills. Distribute envelopes for students to decorate as wallets to store their Bunny Money. Take along a "lucky quarter" to call Grandma—just like Max did. Label an empty oatmeal container with the words *Bunny Money* to collect the money as it is spent in the story. Convert a toy cash register into an ATM. After filling it with the Bunny Money, let each student punch in fifteen dollars and remove one five-dollar bill and ten one-dollar bills. It's helpful to have a volunteer on hand to monitor the transactions.

Now children are ready to go shopping with Max and Ruby as shown in the mini-lesson that follows.

Mrs. L.:	Would you like to go shopping with Max and Ruby today?
Leah:	You mean shopping for Grandma's birthday present?
Mrs. L.:	I think they could use our help.
Kelly:	I didn't bring any money with me.
Mrs. L.:	We'd better go to the bank first and get some money—
Kevin:	In case Max spends the bus money!
Mrs. L.:	Good thinking. Let's look on the opening page where Ruby is holding open her wallet. Count with me to find out how much money she has to spend. We'll take the same amount with us.
Wyatt:	I remember she had one five-dollar bill.
Mrs. L.:	Right. Let's count the ones together.
Class:	One, two, three, four, five, six, seven, eight, nine, ten.

Getting Bunny Money at the ATM

Mrs. L.:	So we need five plus ten dollars. Let's add on starting with five. I'll point to the dollar bills while you count.
Class:	Five, six, seven, eight, nine, ten, eleven, twelve, thirteen, fourteen, fifteen.
Wyatt:	We need to take fifteen dollars.
Mrs. L.:	Great! Let's see if fifteen dollars will be enough money for our shopping trip with Max and Ruby. Let's get in line at the cash machine for some Bunny Money.
Joni:	Why is a cash machine called an ATM machine?
Mrs. L.:	ATM stands for automated teller machine. A machine gives you money instead of a real teller.
Kelly:	It's the machine where you swipe your card, punch in a few numbers to tell how much money you want, and the money comes right out of the machine.
Mrs. L.:	You'll need to punch in the number fifteen to get your cash for our shopping trip. (While some groups of students make their withdrawals, have others decorate their envelope wallets.)
Mrs. L.:	I think we're ready to go shopping! Look at the first page where Ruby is holding her wallet. Tell me something about the way her money is arranged.
Lucy:	All the bunny ears are pointing the same way.
Mrs. L.:	You're right! I didn't notice that before. Tell me more.
Tara:	She has the numbers all poking out of her wallet so she can see them better.
Mrs. L.:	Yes, she does. Do you notice anything else?
Tyler:	She has the five first and then all the ones next.
Marc:	That way she knows where the five is. It's sort of hidden since it's worth a lot of Bunny Money.
Mrs. L.:	She seems very organized, doesn't she! You may take a minute to arrange the money in your wallet to look like Ruby's, if you like. Now, let's read the story.

(I read the story aloud in its entirety. The sentences below in italics highlight the sentences in which Max and Ruby spend their Bunny Money.)

Mrs. L.: Ruby took one dollar from her wallet to pay the bus fare. I'll pass around a can for you to put your bus fare in. How much money is left in your wallet? Start with the five, and count on.

Class: Five, six, seven, eight, nine, ten, eleven, twelve, thirteen, fourteen dollars.

Brian: Not for long. Look! Ruby hands Max the wallet on this page! That's a mistake.

Mrs. L.: Uh-oh. I'll continue reading. I think we're almost at the gift shop.

The bus stopped at Rosalinda's Gift Shop . . .

"Thirsty," said Max.

"You may buy a very, very small lemonade, Max," said Ruby.

Next door in Candi's Corner window were hundreds of vampire teeth.

Max knew Grandma would love a set of teeth with oozing cherry syrup inside for her birthday.

He bought them instead of the lemonade.

"Two dollars, please," said Candi.

Put two dollars in this can for Candi, please. Now how much money do you have left? Start counting with the five-dollar bill. Then add on the ones.

Class: Five, six seven, eight, nine, ten, eleven, twelve. Twelve dollars.

Jason: Oh, no! We'd better buy the gift fast. We're running out of money!

Mrs. L.: I'll keep reading. *Max wanted to make sure the teeth worked. He put them in. The teeth worked perfectly . . . Ruby had to take him to the—*

Class: Laundromat.

Kelly: And it's expensive!

Mrs. L.: *Soap cost a dollar. The washer cost a dollar. And the dryer cost another dollar. "Money down the drain, Max," said Ruby.* How much money did Max and Ruby spend at the Laundromat?

Jordan: Three whole dollars!

Kevin: One for the washer, one for the dryer, and one for soap.

Mrs. L.: Please put three dollars in the can. How much do you have left? Start with the five and then add on the ones.

Class: Five, six, seven, eight, nine!

Mrs. L.: We had twelve dollars, we spent three dollars. That leaves nine because twelve take away three is nine. What happens next?

Kyle: Max gets hungry, I bet.

Mrs. L.: *It was lunchtime. Max finished off a peanut butter and jelly sandwich, two cupcakes, and a banana shake. Lunch cost four dollars.* Uh-oh! Now how much do you have left?

Leah: Only the five-dollar bill! Lunch used up all our ones!

Mrs. L.: *"Money is running through our fingers, Max," said Ruby. They walked all the way back to Rosalinda's Gift Shop without spending another penny.*

Tyler: But she can't buy the music box because the feet are made of real gold, and it costs one hundred dollars.

Mrs. L.:	That's a lot of Bunny Money! I'll keep reading. *Ruby looked in her wallet. The only thing left was a five-dollar bill. "Here's an idea!" said Rosalinda. "Bluebird earrings that play 'Oh, What a Beautiful Morning!' are on sale for four dollars. Gift wrap is free." "We'll take them," said Ruby.*
Tara:	But she doesn't have four dollars, she has a five-dollar bill.
Brian:	That's okay. Five is more than four so she'll get change.
Mrs. L.:	I'll show you how it works. This five-dollar bill is the same as five one-dollar bills. *(I hold up the five in Bunny Money.)* Help me count this five-dollar bill.
Class:	Five.
Mrs. L.:	Great! *(I hold up the five ones in Bunny Money.)* Help me count the ones.
Class:	One, two, three, four, five.
Mrs. L.:	Excellent. You see, we made five dollars in two ways. Now, the bluebird earrings cost four dollars. Help me count four dollars for Ruby to give to Rosalinda.
Class:	One, two, three, four.
Mrs. L.:	How many dollar bills do I have left?
Class:	One.
Mrs. L.:	Right. *"Four dollars for the earrings . . . one dollar change!" said Rosalinda. "You take care of this dollar, young man!" Max went back to Candi's Corner. Glow-in-the-dark vampire teeth were half price . . . Max bought a set for one dollar.*
Wyatt:	That's our last dollar!
Mrs. L.:	I'll take it for Candi, thank you.
Wyatt:	How will we get home?
Mrs. L.:	*"Oh, no, Max," said Ruby. "You've spent our last dollar. How are we going to pay for the bus home?" Max reached into his pocket. Out came his lucky quarter. Ruby used it for the telephone.*
Joni:	We don't have a quarter.
Mrs. L.:	I do. *(I reach into my pocket and place my "lucky quarter" in the can).* "Grandma will have to pick us up," said Ruby. "I hope she won't be angry."
Amy:	She's not. She drives home wearing the earrings and the candy teeth.
Mrs. L.:	I'm glad Grandma liked her presents from Max and Ruby. Her birthday turned out to be an expensive shopping adventure.
Renee:	Yes, but we didn't spend all the money on Grandma.
Mrs. L.:	Let's make a list of what we bought. I'll pass out the money to you as you name each thing it was spent on.

Then, to close the lesson, I ask the children to draw a picture of how they would spend their Bunny Money if they could use it like real money.

More Must-Have Books To Count On

Chicken Soup with Rice
by Maurice Sendak

 **LEARNING ABOUT** **Time (Months/Calendars)**

In January
it's so nice
while slipping
on the sliding ice
to sip hot chicken soup
with rice.
Sipping once
sipping twice
sipping chicken soup
with rice.

— From *Chicken Soup with Rice*, page 6

In this clever, classic rhyming book of months, Maurice Sendak convinces readers that every month is right for sipping chicken soup with rice. Kick off the new year and minimize the winter blahs by adding a *Chicken Soup with Rice* celebration in January. Incorporated into your daily calendar routine, this short and snappy rhyme of the months provides a fun and effective way for kindergarten children to learn the months of the year.

Place Popsicle sticks labeled with individual students' names in an empty chicken soup with rice can (use a glue gun to attach a strip of felt around the edges of the can to prevent cuts to little hands). Display the names of the months near your class calendar. Each day during calendar time, select a name from the can. This student becomes the Chicken Soup with Rice Helper of the Day.

Using a pointer, the student helper points to each month of the year as the rest of the class recites Sendak's poem with you. Although some children will memorize the entire poem by heart, others will join in on the "sipping once, sipping twice, sipping chicken soup with rice" lines that change with each new month; in March, when the wind blows, the words become "blowing once, blowing twice, blowing chicken soup with rice." After sharing the book in class, the Helper of the Day gets to take the little book home to share with parents.

MORE FUN WITH THE BOOK

Ask parents to donate cans of chicken soup with rice. Each time a student is able to name the months in order from January to December, a can is placed in a box to be donated to a local food bank in honor of that student. Once all the students have made an effort to learn the months of the year, hold a Chicken Soup with Rice celebration—perhaps take a bus to the food bank to deliver the cans of soup and then return to school in time for a snack of canned chicken soup with rice.

Miss Bindergarten Celebrates the 100th Day of Kindergarten
by Joseph Slate

LEARNING ABOUT   ## Counting To 100

Let this story inspire your class to anticipate and prepare for a 100th Day Celebration of their own—just like Miss Bindergartener's kindergartners. Keep track of your days in school, and remind students that you will have a 100th day of kindergarten celebration that is bound to be unforgettable! (***Note:*** See Chapter 4 of Math Their Way Summary Newsletter, Center for Innovation in Education, 1988, to learn how to incorporate the calendar activities portrayed in Miss Bindergarten's kindergarten class into your everyday routine.)

To activate students' anticipation of the 100th day, read aloud this must-have book early in the year and revisit it often. On the 100th day of school, take Miss Bindergarten's lead and introduce as many of her ideas as possible into your celebration. Of course, you'll want to kick off the day with a rereading of *Miss Bindergarten Celebrates the 100th Day of Kindergarten*. Plan ahead as carefully as Miss Bindergarten does, and your kindergarten's 100th-day centers should go off without a hitch.

100 One-Hundred-Full Collections

Just as Miss Bindergarten does on the opening page, send a note home asking students to bring in a collection of 100 of some wonderful, one-hundred-full thing. Those students who forget to do their homework may count out a collection of 100 things from the classroom when they arrive in the morning. Display their collections around the room for others to count during free time. And don't forget your own collection—Miss Bindergarten pinned 100 bows on her dress!

Rich Vocabulary

dazzling *adj.* bright

delay *v.* to wait until later

I Could Eat 100 Things

Challenge students to draw posters with the following title: I Could Eat 100 _____.
Display their work in the classroom as illustrated on pages 18–19 of the book.

100th-Day Heavenly Hash

This original concoction is a favorite of students but be prepared to have extra on hand as a few nibblers can deplete your hash rations in no time. Set out individual bowls filled with cereal o's, pretzels, marshmallows, nuts, raisins, sunflower seeds, chocolate chips, cereal "pillows," and popcorn. Direct students to pick 10 items from each bowl to make their own hash.

100th-Day Punch

Follow the recipe for a simple yet special 100th-day drink: Miss Bindergarten's refreshing drink calls for 10 cans of lemon-lime soda, 100 ice cubes, and 100 cherries. Assign pairs of students a counting task such as adding a can of soda, adding 10 ice cubes or 10 cherries to the punch bowl. After read-aloud, pour the punch, and give 100 hip-hip hoorays for the 100th day!

100th-Day Hats

Have students make newspaper hats (like Coco the bird's shown on the book cover) as Miss Bindergarten directs on page 14 at the make a hat center. Or make simple, cone-shaped party hats with chin strings. Challenge students to make 100 tallies on their hats and circle each group of 10 tallies.

Hang 100 Hearts

Deck the hall with 100 number messages as illustrated on page 26. Start jotting down the ideas well before the 100th day of school. Urge the class to think of a number message for every number from 1 to 100, and then surprise them by hanging the notes for the 100th day.

100th-Day Memory Book

Have each child contribute a page for a class book to remember the 100th day of school. Use the examples on pages 38–39 of the book. Ask students to illustrate and dictate a description of their collection of 100 things. Add a cover page, and place in a binder for students to enjoy during silent reading time.

More Great Books About Miss Bindergarten and Her Kindergarten

Miss Bindergarten Gets Ready for Kindergarten

Miss Bindergarten Stays Home from Kindergarten

Miss Bindergarten Takes a Field Trip with Kindergarten

Miss Bindergarten Plans a Circus with Kindergarten

12 Ways to Get to 11
by Eve Merriam

Number Sense

ONE, TWO
THREE, FOUR,
FIVE, SIX,
SEVEN, EIGHT,
NINE, TEN,

TWELVE.
WHERE'S ELEVEN?

— From *12 Ways to Get to 11*, pages 6–7

> ### Rich Vocabulary
>
> **darting** *v.* moving quickly

Eleven is missing. Where can it be? In this book, which Horn Book described as "fun, lively and painlessly educational," children are presented with 12 sets of different objects that, when placed together, make 11. Nine pine cones from the forest floor and 2 acorns make 11; 6 peanuts and 5 pieces of popcorn at the circus make 11, too. Readers peek inside a magician's hat, go on a boat, visit a farm, and look inside the mailbox for a few of the 12 ways to get to 11.

Perfect for developing number sense, introducing addition skills, and counting, this book encourages practical math thinking that is fun and painless. Share this book for read-aloud, stop to count the objects on each page, and then ask, "How can you get to 11?"

Invite students to look around the classroom and name objects that become 11 when they are placed together. Throughout the day, challenge students to think of 12 different ways to make 11. Record their ideas using simple pictures.

Our 12 Ways to Get to 11

1. 5 ponytails + 3 sets of pig tails
2. 3 red blocks + 2 yellow blocks + 6 green blocks
3. 7 noses + 2 pairs of eyes
4. 4 kids at the yellow table + 4 kids at the green table + 3 kids at the red table
5. 6 swings + 4 balls + 1 jump rope at recess
6. 4 pretzels + 4 carrots + 1 milk carton + 2 sandwich halves
7. 1 cupcake + 3 cookies + 2 Goldfish crackers + 5 grapes
8. 9 pencils + 2 erasers
9. 5 crayons + 6 markers
10. 3 coats + 3 hats + 3 boots + 2 mittens
11. 1 square house + 1 door + 4 windows + 1 chimney + 1 triangle roof + 2 trees + 1 sun
12. The sentence, "This is my dog": 4 letters + 2 letters + 2 letters + 3 letters

MORE FUN WITH THE BOOK

Ways to Get to 11 Center: Set up a center where students make designs of 11 with different objects. Pattern blocks, buttons with different size holes, shapes, or macaroni glued onto paper; stacks of Unifix cubes, and blocks, all make fun ways for exploring the number 11.

Painted Beans: Spread a bag of dry navy beans onto a large sheet of butcher block paper. Paint one side of the beans with blue spray paint, and let dry. For an independent practice activity, give pairs of students 11 blue-and-white beans in a paper cup. Direct partners to take turns shaking the cup of beans and dumping them onto a table. They sort the beans into a pile of blue beans and a pile of white beans and then record the way they made 11.

Our designs for 11

TEACHING TIP

Assessing Number Sense

This technique of building an awareness of number sense works well for all numbers from 1 to 10. On subsequent days, identify a number of the day for students to find in the world around them. Two, for example, is found in pairs of eyes, ears, shoes, mittens, socks, and so on. What about 3? Wheels on a tricycle, the number of books that can be checked out at the library, perhaps, or the number of teeth lost between or among friends.

For a quick one-on-one assessment of number sense or which numbers individuals have mastered, place 1 to 5 counters (or beans, buttons, erasers, or other small objects) in your hand. Ask students to name the number without actually counting. Repeat for each number from 1 to 5 (and then extend learning from 6 to 10). This will give you an idea of mastered numbers and numbers to practice during independent work times.

....

One of Each
by Mary Ann Hoberman

 **Equal Parts**

In the one little kitchen was one little sink
And one little cupboard all shiny and pink,

And inside the cupboard one pear and one peach,
One plum and one apple, just one, one of each.

One plum and one apple, one pear and one peach.
Just one, only one, simply one, one of each.
— From *One of Each*, pages 6–7

Rich Vocabulary

arranged *v.* placed in a certain order

glee *n.* a feeling of happiness

One glimpse of the cover of *One of Each*, and I couldn't wait to get my hands on this book. Mary Ann Hoberman's rhyming text extolling the joys of sharing combined with Marjorie Priceman's exuberant illustrations makes this a perfect book for kindergarten read-aloud.

Charming Oliver Tolliver is quite happy with one of each thing until he meets Miss Peggoty Small. Peggoty thinks his collection of one is perfect for one and therefore leaves him alone. Suddenly Oliver Tolliver realizes that one thing was missing—he didn't have one friend. After he buys one more of each thing, one becomes two. Thanks to Peggoty Small, Oliver Tolliver ultimately learns that "two was better than one! Jolly and friendly, more cheerful, more fun!" So when Oliver's one friend turns into seven friends and the cupcakes and tea are gone, he remembers that the cupboard has two of each kind of fruit—apples, peaches, pears, and plums, which he cuts into slices and serves.

Following a read-aloud of the book, teach a math lesson that explores equal parts. Bring in a bag of apples to share. Tell students that you will cut each apple into 8 pieces. Ask: "If I give one piece of apple to each of you, how many apples will I need to cut up?" It may help students to visualize the amount if you line up counters to represent each piece of apple as shown below.

8 pieces of apple

1 apple = ● ● ● ●
          ● ● ● ●

2 apples = ● ● ● ● + ● ● ● ●
            ● ● ● ●   ● ● ● ●

3 apples = ● ● ● ● + ● ● ● ● + ● ● ● ●
            ● ● ● ●   ● ● ● ●   ● ● ● ●

Then cut up the apple, explaining equal parts as you do so. Line up the pieces of apple for counting. Allow students to sample the apple, and count backwards as each student removes a piece of fruit from the line. To extend the activity, ask students how many apples you will need if you cut each into 4 pieces.

ON ANOTHER DAY

Bring in the variety of fruit mentioned in the book, and slice them into equal pieces. End your *One of Each* sharing session by making a graph to record students' favorite fruit.

Blueberries for Sal
by Robert McCloskey

Addition and Subtraction, Counting, Estimation

Little Sal picked three berries and dropped them in her little tin pail . . . kuplink, kuplank, kuplunk!
She picked three more berries and ate them. Then she picked more berries and dropped one in her pail—
kuplunk! And the rest she ate.
Then Little Sal ate all four blueberries out of her pail!
— From *Blueberries for Sal*, pages 6–7

This 1948 Caldecott Honor book should be a part of every child's read-aloud repertoire. When Little Sal and her mother and Little Bear and his mother go blueberry picking on Blueberry Hill, a mix-up occurs that separates the two families among the blueberries on blueberry hill.

Most kindergartners empathize with Little Sal in her struggle to refrain from eating the berries and when she wanders off and loses her Mother. She's a typical child with a mind of her own—not unlike Little Bear.

Have a little math-related fun with *Blueberries for Sal*. Let students use manipulatives to represent blueberries and then add, subtract, count, and estimate in these activities.

Blueberries in the Bucket Addition and Subtraction

Gather a small bucket, blue (or other colored) beads to represent blueberries, and a paper cup "bucket" for each student. Present students with addition and subtraction word problems based on picking and eating blueberries. As you add and take away beads from your bucket, ask students to do the same with their beads and paper-cup buckets.

Little Sal puts 5 blueberries in her bucket—kuplink, kuplank, kuplunk, kuplink, kuplank. She eats 1 blueberry. How many blueberries are left?

There are 4 berries in Little Sal's bucket. She eats 3 berries. How many berries are left?

There is only 1 blueberry in Little Sal's bucket. So she picks 4 more blueberries— kuplink, kuplank, kuplunk, kuplink. How many blueberries are in the bucket now?

Little Sal runs to catch up with her mother. Two berries fall out of her bucket. There are 3 berries left in the bucket. How many blueberries did Little Sal start with?

Rich Vocabulary

hustling *v.* moving quickly

tremendous *adj.* huge

Counting Practice

Have students close their eyes and listen as you drop blueberries (beads) into your bucket. Ask them to count silently and then raise their hands to reveal the number of blueberries in the bucket.

Estimating Blueberries

Set up an estimating and counting center using different-size buckets and containers filled with collections of 1 to 20 objects (dried pasta, beans, beads, counters or buttons of the same size work well). Provide copies of the reproducible on page 61. Ask students to estimate and then count the objects in each bucket.

The Missing Mitten Mystery
by Steven Kellogg

 **LEARNING ABOUT**

Problem-Solving Strategies

Rich Vocabulary

snugly *adv.* comfortably

Math is all about thinking logically in order to solve problems. In *The Missing Mitten Mystery*, Steven Kellogg presents a character who goes through the problem-solving process. Readers are privy to her process as she talks her way through the problem with her dog, Oscar. As Annie works backward through her day of snow play to find her fifth lost mitten of the season, she invents some pretty innovative possibilities. For instance, perhaps she should plant the other mitten in the garden and grow new ones; a sprouting mitten tree would produce plenty of extra mates for the next snowy season! It isn't until a great deal of searching, imagining, and raining that the mitten surfaces as the heart of a snowman.

Read this story to your students to get their imaginations growing, and then have them solve a mystery. Display a box with a removable lid. Explain that you have placed an item from the classroom inside the box. They may ask 20 yes-or-no questions to solve the mystery of what's inside the box. Students will sharpen their problem-solving skills as they learn that asking more generalized questions generate the best answers for solving the mystery: "Is it a boot?" gives a very limited amount of information compared to "Is it brown?"

As students ask questions, keep a tally of the number of questions and a simplified list of the information gathered. After every five questions, stop and review the information gathered. Allow three minutes of discussion for small groups to assimilate information. When groups are confident they have solved the mystery, review the list to see if their ideas fit the criteria of answers. If the answer is yes to all the listed criteria, ask a volunteer to look inside the box to confirm the guess. If the mystery has not been solved after 20 questions and answers, allow students to ask 10 more questions. The sample shown is typical of how one question often leads to the next.

20 QUESTIONS ABOUT OUR MYSTERY BOX

|||| |||| |||| ||||

1. Is it big?	no	**11.** Does it make noise?	no
2. Is it smaller than a book?	yes	**12.** Do you wear it?	yes
3. Can you eat it?	no	**13.** Is it a green shirt?	no
4. Is it red?	no	**14.** Is it a green sock?	no
5. Is it blue?	no	**15.** Does it go on your head?	no
6. Is it green?	yes	**16.** Does it go on your feet? *(wasted question: see #12)*	no
7. Are there any in the room?	yes	**17.** Does it go on your arms?	no
8. Is it something you play with?	no	**18.** Is it a green shoe?	no
9. Is it something you write with?	no	**19.** Does it go on your hands?	yes
10. Is it bumpy?	no	**20.** Is it a pair of green mittens?	yes

ON ANOTHER DAY

For a listening/spatial orientation activity, pass out a sheet of paper with the outline of a mitten to each student. Pair students, and have partners sit back to back. One student is the leader. Using very clear directions, the leader decorates his or her mitten while orally explaining to the partner what he or she is doing. The other partner listens and colors his or her mitten to look exactly like the leader's—without either student peeking. Students compare mittens to see how closely they resemble a matching pair. Distribute more mitten outlines, and have partners reverse roles.

....

Inch by Inch

by Leo Lionni

 **LEARNING ABOUT** **Measuring Length**

In this 1960 Caldecott Honor Book, readers meet an inchworm who outsmarts a robin to avoid becoming its breakfast. The bird and inchworm journey off together to find other birds that need to be measured. From the neck of the flamingo to the entire length of a hummingbird, the inchworm measures and measures until he meets a nightingale who wants his song measured.

> ## Rich Vocabulary
>
> **useful** *adj.* having many ways to be used

Read aloud the story, stopping after pages 21–22.

"Measure my song or I'll eat you for breakfast," said the nightingale.
Then the inchworm had an idea.
"I'll try," he said, "go ahead and sing."

Ask students whether a song could be measured. Discuss possible solutions for the inchworm's dilemma before reading the ending where the clever inchworm makes a wise decision to measure "inch by inch . . . until he inched out of sight."

Let your students gain the confidence that they, too, can measure anything, inch by inch, block by block, link by link, or clip by clip. Set up a center where they can practice measuring length using nonstandard units of measurement.
Any objects of the same size can be used such as Unifix cubes, pattern blocks, paper clips, plastic learning links, and so on. Supply a box of classroom objects for students to measure using these nonstandard units. Show them how to line up their nonstandard units to record the length of an object.

Move from concrete to pictorial representation by handing out copies of the reproducible on page 62. Tell students to color and cut out the inchworm ruler at the bottom of the page. Demonstrate how to measure objects from the box or pictures on the pages of Leo Lionni's book using the ruler. Meet to compare results of students' measurements.

Measuring block by block

. . . .

A Pair of Socks
by Stuart J. Murphy

 **LEARNING ABOUT** **Identifying Patterns**

The concept of patterning, a predominant goal of the kindergarten math curriculum, takes center stage in this *MathStart* book. Two pages of ideas are included to extend the learning of matching and patterning concepts.

On the opening page, a lone red-and-blue striped sock makes a fervent plea for help:

I'll never be worn. It doesn't seem fair.
I'm missing my match—I'm not part of a pair.

Rich Vocabulary

grimy *adj.* very dirty

Slimy, spotted, and other not-quite-alike socks are boldly illustrated by Lois Ehlert's masterful collage technique. The socks complement Stuart J. Murphy's text in a way that is sure to attract readers' attention as they search the pages for the matching sock among the other pairs.

A pair of socks

After read-aloud, have students draw, color, and cut out pairs of socks in matching patterns. Arrange the socks patterned side down, and ask students to select one pair at a time for a game of Match the Socks. To extend the activity, gather matched and mismatched household items such as place mats, shoes, or towels. Ask students to identify the pairs that are different and the same. Apply the idea of patterns to things in the real world such as wallpaper, rugs, shirts, and so on.

MORE FUN WITH THE BOOK

Collage Patterns: Give students an opportunity to explore patterning and Lois Ehlert's collage technique. Provide scrap paper for students to cut and paste designs that match onto a pair of paper socks.

Sock Day: Hold a Sock Day at school. Send a note home inviting students to wear or bring a favorite pair of socks. Ask students to leave their shoes at the door, and sort them by sock patterns—stripes, colors, designs, or characters. You may also ask students to bring a pair of clean matched socks that have a pattern. Drop the socks into a laundry basket, and you've got a center where students can sort socks into pairs for a real-life application of math.

Other MathStart Books by Stuart J. Murphy

A Fair Bear Share illustrated by John Speirs
Monster Musical Chairs illustrated by Scott Nash
Lemonade for Sale illustrated by Tricia Tusa
Missing Mittens illustrated by G. Brian Karas

Katy and the Big Snow
by Virginia Lee Burton

LEARNING ABOUT   **Extending Patterns**

This classic book has been a children's favorite for over 60 years, and it stands up to repeated rereading. The simple and matter-of-fact text is well complemented by detailed illustrations and border pictures that children love to pore over. (When a big blanket of snow covers the city of Geoppolis, the brightly colored illustrations turn mostly white and then become more colorful again as Katy plows the city.)

As you read aloud *Katy and the Big Snow*, share the map of the city of Geoppolis on pages 10 and 11. Compare the places in Geoppolis to places in your own town. Have students tell about the locations that might need the help of a beautiful red crawler tractor with a snowplow—just like Katy—if there was a big snow.

Following your book discussion, have a little patterning fun. Make patterned streets in Geoppolis for Katy to plow. Give each student a strip of adding machine paper to represent Katy's path. Cut shapes from craft foam to make buildings. Explain that in this Geoppolis, there must be a 2- or 3-step pattern to the buildings on each street.

Tape students' streets along the baseboard of one wall in the classroom. Provide a toy bull-dozer or snowplow to represent Katy, and let students use it to plow the streets as they identify the building patterns.

Rich Vocabulary

drifts *n.* piles or mounds of something (snow)

steadily *adv.* without stopping

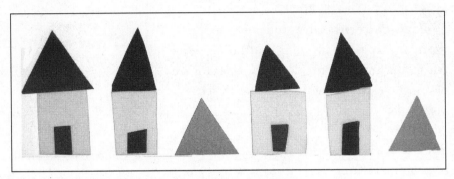

Red door, blue door, tree; red door, blue door, tree . . .

Even More Must-Have Books to Count On

Little Rabbit's First Number Book by Alan Baker

Counting Crocodiles by Judy Sierra

Brown Bear's Shape Book by Alan Baker

When Sheep Cannot Sleep: The Counting Book by Satoshi Kitamura

Anno's Counting Book by Mitsumasa Anno

Five Little Monkeys Sitting in the Tree by Eileen Christelow

Count the Ways, Little Brown Bear by J. London

Let's Count it Out, Jesse Bear by Nancy White Carlstrom

Let's Count by Tana Hoban

Who's Counting by Nancy Tafuri

Frog Jump: A Counting Book by Alan Brooks

Snowy Flowy Blowy: A Twelve Months Rhyme by Nancy Tafuri

The Right Number of Elephants by Jeff Sheppard

I Knew Two Who Said Moo by Judi Barrett

Name _____ Date _____

Happy Counting!

Directions: About how many things are in each bucket? Write your estimate. Then count the objects in each bucket. Write the number of objects.

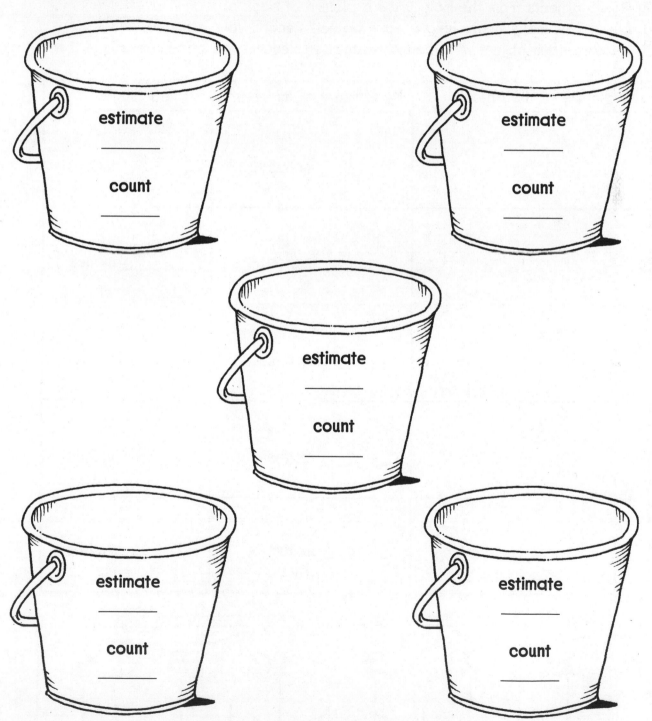

Inchworm Ruler

Directions:

1. Color and cut out the inchworm ruler below.
2. Pick 5 objects from the box. Draw a picture of each object.
3. About how many inches long is each object? Record your estimate.
4. Measure each object with the inchworm ruler. Record how many inches long it is.

My picture of the object	My estimate of its length	Its real length
	_____ inches	_____ inches
	_____ inches	_____ inches
	_____ inches	_____ inches
	_____ inches	_____ inches
	_____ inches	_____ inches

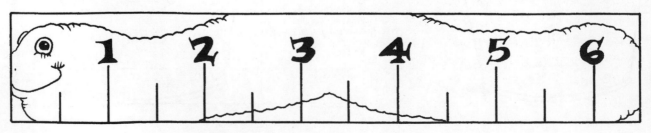

Use with Inch by Inch by Leo Lionni.

Teaching With Favorite Read-Alouds in Kindergarten

Chapter 4: Feeling Good About Me!
10 Must-Have Books for Building Self-Esteem Through Art, Music, and Movement

Chapter Learning Goals:
* building self-confidence
* identifying personal strengths through creative expression
* strengthening fine-motor skills through coloring and cutting activities
* strengthening gross-motor skills by participating in movement activities
* exploring music, art, and movement as forms of self-expression
* developing oral and listening skills

Young children build confidence in themselves by understanding and developing their own unique strengths. To a kindergartner, self-esteem begins with simple accomplishments—buttoning a shirt, zipping a coat, tying shoes, pouring a glass of milk—and it extends to reading, writing, and counting. In these early years, discovering strengths in music, art, and movement can help children feel successful; in turn, this success builds self-confidence. Each step toward success has setbacks and requires perseverance; every day is an adventure in learning more about one's self and one's strengths.

Learn to take pride in everyday accomplishments in *I'm Gonna Like Me*. Get carried away with one's artistic side in *Purple, Green and Yellow*, and use art to make cards that say *Happy Birthday, Moon*. Sing a song to *Make Way for Ducklings*. Express emotions through movement with *Caps for Sale*. Try out a variety of movements *From Head to Toe*. Create instruments and form a band to make *Music, Music for Everyone*. Get innovative with *Arthur's TV Trouble*. Pantomime movement to *The Little Mouse, the Red Ripe Strawberry, and THE BIG HUNGRY BEAR*. Play a listening game as you *Whistle for Willie*. Read this chapter of great books to get students moving, singing, painting and more through art, music, and movement.

10 Must-Have Books for Building Self-Esteem Through Art, Music, and Movement

I'm Gonna Like Me: Letting Off a Little Self-Esteem by Jamie Lee Curtis and Laura Cornell

Purple, Green and Yellow by Robert Munsch

Make Way for Ducklings by Robert McCloskey

Happy Birthday, Moon by Frank Asch

Caps for Sale by Esphyr Slobodkina

From Head to Toe by Eric Carle

Music, Music for Everyone by Vera B. Williams

Arthur's TV Trouble by Marc Brown

The Little Mouse, the Red Ripe Strawberry, and THE BIG HUNGRY BEAR by Don and Audrey Wood

Whistle for Willie by Ezra Jack Keats

I'm Gonna Like Me:
Letting Off a Little Self-Esteem

by Jamie Lee Curtis and Laura Cornell

LEARNING ABOUT Celebrating Personal Strengths

I'm gonna like me
when I jump out of bed,
from my giant big toe
to the braids on my head.
— From *I'm Gonna Like Me*, pages 4-5

The subtitle to this whimsical book says it all. Letting off steam makes us feel better on a bad day. Letting off a little self-esteem makes every day more positive. Plant the idea in your students' minds that liking yourself is the key to feeling good about you— whoever you are. Through good times and bad, the boy and girl in this book declare, "I'm gonna like me!" They extol the virtues of letting off self-esteem—and their positive self-image is contagious.

Share this book for read-aloud, and invite students to pore over the pictures as you read the main text. Read the story again, pausing to read the words in the illustrations that add humor to the book. Learn about the boy's interest in firefighting. Highlight the words on the Dalmatian kit, for example, which claim to "make any pet a fireman's best friend." Giggles will erupt with the discovery on the next page that the grimacing cat with taped-on spots is holding a can of "spot remover." There are "cavity extinguisher" toothpaste, a tool belt that organizes "Mr. Wrench, Mr. Scissors, Mr. Flashlight, and Mr. Magnifying Glass," and sticky notes around the house warning of fire hazards.

Rich Vocabulary

style *n.* your own way of doing things

task *n.* job

Learn about the girl's interests by her reading choices including *Trucker Gal* and *Exercising your Illegal Turtle*. Discover her desire to become a nurse from the box of "nurse shoes through the ages," her Clara Barton book, and her nurse's hat and cape. The collection of wearable fins and "bonus attachable fins" worn by her dog, are sure to entertain kindergartners.

In our reading of *I'm Gonna Like Me*, self-esteem permeates our classroom as we compare the unique qualities of the characters with those things that make us special; in doing so, we celebrate each other. Join my students and me for a discussion of the lively illustrations and triumphant text that allow us to let off a little self-esteem. Have copies of the puppet reproducible on page 77 and tongue depressors ready to distribute following a brief discussion of the opening pages of smiling children.

Mrs. L.:	Repeat after me: I like me!
Class:	I like me!
Mrs. L.:	Say it again—louder this time.
Class:	I like me!
Mrs. L.:	It feels good to say that, doesn't it? The key to feeling good is liking yourself. Like the boy and girl in the story, even when we make mistakes, get embarrassed, lose a tooth, can't run fast, or wear flowers and plaid, we must learn to accept our strengths and differences. These are the things that make us special. Since you spend more time with you than anyone else, today we're going to celebrate with an I'm Gonna Like Me Day. Let's begin by looking at the inside page of the book.
Lauren:	That's a lot of kid's faces.
Kyle:	But they're all different.
Mrs. L.:	They are, but they all have one thing in common.
Joni:	They like themselves. That's why they're in a book called *I'm Gonna Like Me*.
Mrs. L.:	How can you tell they like themselves?
Joni:	They're all smiling.
Mrs. L.:	Excellent. Since "I Like Me" is our theme today, the first thing I'd like you to do is to make a puppet face to look like you—wearing a big smile, of course. Color and cut out the face on the page I handed out. If you have blue eyes, color the eyes on the picture of you blue. Add hair like yours and any other details you can.
Marc:	I wear glasses like the boy in the book.
Mrs. L.:	You can add them like the illustrator Laura Cornell did for this little boy. *(We briefly discuss how the faces can be adapted to students in our class—long blonde hair, glasses, hair decorations, straight versus curly hair, smiles with and without teeth, and so on.)*
Mrs. L.:	When you've decorated your face, please cut it out. Glue your face to a wooden stick to make a puppet of you! We'll meet back at our gathering space to share our puppets and reread *I'm Gonna Like Me*—to let off a little self-esteem.

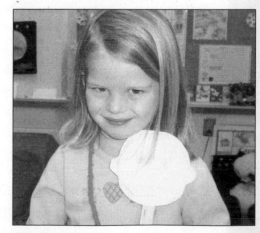

I'm gonna like me!

Mrs. L.:	It's nice to see so many happy, smiling puppet faces. Get your puppets ready for a rereading of *I'm Gonna Like Me*. Take a look at the words on the first two pages.
Tara:	The ones on the second page are fancier.
Leah:	The boy's page has letters like we make.
Renee:	The girl's page is cursive. My sister writes in cursive because she's in third grade.
Mrs. L.:	I think Jamie Lee Curtis wants to show who is talking so she makes a different letter style for each character. When the boy talks—
Gary:	She prints like us.
Mrs. L.:	When the girl talks—
Amy:	It's in fancy letters.
Mrs. L.:	Girls, hold up your puppets when the girl is talking. Boys, hold up your puppets when the boy is talking. Boys, get your puppets ready. "I'm gonna like me when I jump out of bed, from my giant big toe—"
Grant:	His big toe is really big. That makes him special.
Tyler:	I like my toes!
Mrs. L.:	Wave your puppet high in the air if you like your toes. *(I continue reading.)*
Lauren:	This is where the girl starts talking: "to the braids on my head."
Jordan:	Those braids all over the girl's head look funny.
Tara:	I only wear two braids at a time, but she should wear her hair the way she likes it best.
Mrs. L.:	I agree. Wave your puppet in the air if you agree that what we like is one of the things that makes us special. *(Then I continue to read.)* "I'm gonna like me when I grin and I see the space in my mouth where two teeth used to be."
Amy:	I lost my two teeth like that.
Mrs. L.:	And that makes you special, doesn't it?
Amy:	It means I'm growing up. That makes me happy.
Mrs. L.:	Raise your puppet high in the air if you have ever had a space in your mouth where two teeth used to be. Wow! I'll keep reading. "I'm gonna like me wearing flowers and plaid. I have my own style. I don't follow some fad."
Renee:	She doesn't match very well.
Tara:	The colors do. She likes it, so she's going to wear it that way.
Leah:	I think she's playing dress up—
Renee:	No, when you turn the page, she's on the bus going to school like that.
Andrea:	The boy wears his fire hat everywhere.
Tyler:	Nobody else on the bus is wearing dress-up clothes.
Jordan:	Maybe that's why those two are such good friends. They both like to dress up.
Kelly:	When I was little, I wore my ballerina tutu everywhere. My mom washed it every day, and when we'd go somewhere, she let me keep it on under my clothes.
Mrs. L.:	That was a good compromise. I did the same thing with my daughter, Maddie. She wanted to wear her bathing suit in February so I let her wear it around the house, but when we went somewhere, she had to put her clothes over it. I was proud of her for expressing her independence. I also like that she isn't afraid to be different. As a teacher, I think the next two pages are my

Teaching With Favorite Read-Alouds in Kindergarten

favorite: "I'm gonna like me when I'm called on to stand. I know all my letters like the back of my hand."

Wyatt:	I know my letters, too.
Mrs. L.:	Wave your puppet in the air if you know all the letters.
Paul:	I'll wave mine a little. Sometimes I get *U* and *W* mixed up . . . and little *b* and *d*.
Mrs. L.:	You should be proud of yourself for the letters you do know already.
Kelly:	And try and try again with the rest.
Mrs. L.:	Exactly. We all learn different things at different times, when we're ready.
Jordan:	When my brain is ready to learn how to read words, it'll read them, right?
Mrs. L.:	Right. Let's read what the little boy has to say: "I'm gonna like me when my answer is wrong, like thinking my ruler was ten inches long."
Lauren:	I get confused about the numbers after ten sometimes, too.
Mrs. L.:	But you're practicing and getting better all the time.
Tara:	You shouldn't laugh at someone when they make a mistake.
Mrs. L.:	That's a very important manner to remember. And you feel good inside when you make others feel good about themselves.
Lucy:	It feels nice to help people and make them happy.
Mrs. L.:	I agree. Let's see what else we have in common with the little boy and girl in the story. *(We continue reading, discussing, and comparing similarities and differences among ourselves and the book characters.)*
Mrs. L.:	It's important to say good things about yourself, to feel good about yourself and to let off a little self-esteem. Let me read the last page: "I'm gonna like me. I already do! But enough about me—How about you?" How about you? Take a minute to think about how you would finish this idea: I'm gonna like me when . . .

At the end of the day, I send home a note asking parents to help children choose a silly or favorite picture of themselves. We use them to make an I'm Gonna Like Me bulletin board with a collage of puppets and pictures. I also include snapshots taken throughout our I'm Gonna Like Me Day. Each student dictates a line to finish the I'm Gonna Like Me When . . . story starter on a chart as shown below.

I'm Gonna Like Me When . . .

I use too much syrup on my pancakes and it drips on the floor.

I forget to turn off the water in the bathtub before it hits the floor.

I accidentally open the door and let my dog out and he runs away. (We found him.)

I move to a new place where I don't know anybody.

I share with my brother (or sister).

I read a word all by myself.

I run really fast.

My cat gives me kisses.

I give somebody a present that I'd really like to keep for myself.

I leave my favorite ball in the yard and my dog eats it.

I make a picture that my Mom likes so much she puts it in a frame.

More Must-Have Books for Building Self-Esteem Through Art, Music, and Movement

....

Purple, Green and Yellow
by Robert Munsch

Self-Expression Through Coloring

. . . "Mommy, I need some colouring markers."
"Oh no!" said her mother. "I've heard about those colouring markers. Kids draw on walls, they draw on the floor, they draw on themselves. You can't have any colouring markers."
— From *Purple, Green and Yellow*, page 3

Young children relate to Brigid's desire to try the new markers that "all her friends have"; they understand why she gets tired of drawing only on paper. Not wanting to draw on the walls or the floor, Brigid draws on her fingernails and ends up drawing all the way to her bellybutton—unfortunately, she does so with the "super-indelible-never-come-off-till-you're-dead-and-maybe-even-later colouring markers."

Read the story to your class as they giggle at Brigid's clever solution to her self-created problem and the delightful ending. Then break out the markers, and allow students to do a little drawing of their own!

Lauren colors her hands.

To promote self expression as well as strengthen fine-motor skills, invite students to color a picture based on the story. If possible, bring in some markers that "smell like roses and lemons and oranges" but be sure to hide the indelible ones (and perhaps the markers that smell like "cow plops").

You can offer the choice of coloring on the floor or walls (covered with paper) and on hands (traced on paper). Revisit a few of the pictures from the book to stimulate imaginations and get ideas flowing.

Rich Vocabulary

amazed *adj.* surprised

indelible *adj.* can't be removed

Make Way for Ducklings
by Robert McCloskey

LEARNING ABOUT Self Expression Through Movement

Make way for ducklings coming through town! Michael the police officer plants himself in the middle of the street to let the eight ducklings and their mother cross safely. Then he calls headquarters for backup.

This classic Caldecott book (1941) is a must-read for kindergarten; it contains just the right amount of suspense and a happy ending for all. Share the book, and then talk about what it must have been like crossing a busy street from the duckling's perspective. Point out the way Robert McCloskey portrays each duckling's unique way of crossing the street: the first duck is very attentive; the last one quacks and struggles to keep up with his siblings; and all eight ducklings waddle across the street on feet better suited for ponds than a busy city.

After discussing this great book, we sing the song "8 Little Ducks" to the tune of "6 Little Ducks" in honor of Jack, Kack, Lack, Mack, Nack, Ouack, Pack, and Quack. Chart the new version of the song as shown below.

8 Little Ducks
8 Little Ducks that I once knew,
Fast ones, slower ones, silly ones, too,
But the one little duck with the feather on his back,
He led the others with a quack, quack, quack,
Quack, quack, quack, quack, quack, quack,
He led the others with a quack, quack, quack.

Everyone sings the song while eight students at a time are chosen to be the eight little ducks quack, quack, quacking around the room. Encourage your "little ducks" to develop their own unique ways of walking and quacking around the room.

Rich Vocabulary

enormous *adj.* huge

responsibility *n.* being in charge of certain things

Happy Birthday, Moon
by Frank Asch

LEARNING ABOUT

Self Expression Through Painting

This great book depicting Bear's birthday celebration with the moon combines simple text with bold illustrations. Bear's play on words delights kindergartners who find humor in his excitement as he "talks back and forth with 'Moon.'" From the top of the mountain, Bear's own echo convinces him that he and the moon share a birthday. After exchanging presents, losing the presents, and confirming that they still love each other anyway, Bear and Moon say "Happy Birthday" to each other on the last page.

Following our read-aloud of this book, Kyle suggested that we make birthday cards for the moon to hang facing outward on the windows. "The moon will see our cards tonight," he convincingly told his classmates. We revisited the book, this time looking closely at the illustrations so individuals could get ideas for Happy Birthday, Moon cards of their own.

Designing a birthday card for the Moon

Rich Vocabulary

reply *n.* answer; *v.* to answer

Have students use blue, yellow, dark brown, light brown, green, and black paint to produce cards for the moon. After the paint dries, outline the shapes in the picture to mirror Frank Asch's painting technique. Exploring Asch's technique allows students to explore art as a form of self-expression. The impressive results boosted the self-esteem of many of my young artists.

Caps for Sale
by Esphyr Slobodkina

LEARNING ABOUT

Listening and Movement Skills

Once there was a peddler who sold caps. But he was not like an ordinary peddler carrying his wares on his back. He carried them on top of his head . . .
— From *Caps for Sale*, page 7

This classic tale of a peddler and some monkey business delights young audiences with its humor, suspense, simplicity, and predictability. When the peddler journeys to the countryside to sell his caps, he stops for a rest beneath a tree. He wakes to find his caps missing—all except his own cap.

When you share this book with students, stop after reading the following text on page 23: "Then he looked up in the tree. And what do you think he saw?" Children who know the story will be quick to tell the others about the hat-wearing monkeys on the next page. Continue reading, and listen to children giggle as the monkeys imitate the peddler's frustration. From shaking his finger and then both hands to stamping one foot and then both feet, the monkeys' tsz, tsz, tsz's finally get the best of the peddler. In a last act of desperation, he throws his own cap to the ground and begins to walk away. Luckily, he sees his caps flying to the ground as the monkeys perform one last imitation. The peddler puts the caps back on his head and walks away saying, "Caps! Caps for sale! Fifty cents a cap!"

Give students a chance to explore movement and hone listening skills as they play The Peddler Says, a game based on Simon Says. Choose one student to be the Peddler who gives directions to the Monkeys (the rest of the class). When the Peddler says, "The Peddler says stomp one foot," for example, the Monkeys stomp one foot. Monkeys who perform an action at the wrong time must sit down. The last Monkey standing becomes the Peddler in the next round.

MORE FUN WITH THE BOOK

- Count the caps along with the peddler.
- Teach one-to-one correspondence using paper cutouts of monkeys and caps.
- Have students make caps at the art center. Count 50 pennies to buy caps from classroom peddlers selling their caps.
- Follow up with a read-aloud of *Circus Caps for Sale* by Esphyr Slobodkina. Then enjoy some math fun with the book.

Rich Vocabulary

disturb *v.* to bother

peddler *n.* person who sells things

From Head to Toe
by Eric Carle

LEARNING ABOUT   Exploring Movement

The following words from the back cover of *Head to Toe* speak volumes about the works by favorite author Eric Carle:

"Not only can children listen, imagine, discover, feel and think, but now they can also be a part of the action. It is as if Eric Carle has again reached out and in his special way said, 'Come play with me.'" — Dr. Marianne Torbert, The Leonard Gordon Institute for Human Development Through Play

Let your students express themselves and strengthen gross motor skills by moving from head to toe as they play with Eric Carle. They'll be turning heads, bending necks, wriggling hips, stomping feet, and wiggling toes with the animal hosts of this playful book. From creative movement, identifying body parts, and a follow-up art activity, this book gets a great deal of mileage in a kindergarten classroom.

Read the book, pausing after a few pages to let students join in with the "Can you do it? I can do it!" pattern that repeats throughout the story.

> I am a penguin
> and I turn my head.
> Can you do it?
> I can do it!
> — From *Head to Toe*, pages 2–3

After reading the final page, where the boy tells the parrot he can wiggle his toe, give children a chance to show others what they can do by filling in the blanks with ideas of their own.

> I am <u>Rebecca</u> and I <u>clap</u> my <u>hands</u>. Can you do it?
> I am <u>Andrew</u> and I <u>jump</u> on one <u>foot</u>. Can you do it?

The rest of the class mimics the action and responds as the parrot did by saying, "I can do it! I can do it!"

On successive rereadings, invite children to stand and perform the animal actions as you read the story. Next give students a chance to add their own animal actions to the parade. Here are some suggestions from my class.

> I am a dog and I wag my tail. Can you do it?
> I am a mouse and I twitch my nose. Can you do it?
> I am an alligator and I snap my mouth. Can you do it?
> I am a raccoon and I wash my face. Can you do it?
> I am a fish and I pucker my lips. Can you do it?
> I am a bear and I scratch my back on a tree. Can you do it?
> I am a lizard and I flick my tongue. Can you do it?
> I am an elephant and I stomp my foot. Can you do it?

ON ANOTHER DAY

Set up an art center where students can explore Eric Carle's cut-and-paste collage technique. Have students select an animal from the book. Challenge them to use one of these techniques.

- Draw and cut out a head, arms, legs, feet, hands, and tail from pieces of construction paper. Features can be added with markers or paper scraps. Provide brass paper fasteners for students to use to assemble their animals. These paper animals can move from head to toe during future rereadings of the book.

Gary's bear can move its arms and legs.

- Finger paint an animal on white paper. Revisit the book for a discussion to guess what Eric Carle may have used to give texture to the different animals' coats. How did he make lines for the gorilla's hair? How did he create the marbled effect on the penguin and the seal? After the paint dries, students can cut out body shapes and assemble as described above.

More Must-Have Books by Eric Carle

The Very Busy Spider

Little Cloud

Papa, Can You Please Get the Moon for Me

The Very Quiet Cricket

"Slowly, Slowly, Slowly," said the Sloth

Music, Music for Everyone
by Vera B. Williams

LEARNING ABOUT **Self Expression Through Music**

I put my fingers on the keys and buttons of my accordion.
Jenny tucked her fiddle under her chin.
Mae put her flute to her mouth.
Leora held up her drums.
After that we played and played.
We made mistakes, but we played like a real band.
— From *Music, Music for Everyone*, page 26

The family's big money jar is empty. It had been too heavy to lift before they bought the chair for mother and more than half full when they bought the accordion. Now the jar is empty because Grandma is ill, and Mother must spend all the money to take care of her. In this sequel to *A Chair for My Mother*, the girls form The Oak Street Band to help fill the big money jar again.

Let your students form small bands of their own and put their musical appreciation and expression to the test. Make musical instruments, or borrow some from the music teacher. Have groups prepare an original song or a favorite song and then perform for the rest of the class. If you wish, take the show on the road and set up performances for other classes.

After the performances, talk about how it feels to be in front of an audience. Remind the class how the girls in the book felt until Grandma whispered for them to play like they used to play for her. How would it make students feel to see people dancing to their music, clapping for their efforts, and asking them to play again?

Rich Vocabulary

accordion *n.* a musical instrument

introduce *v.* to meet for the first time

Arthur's TV Trouble
by Marc Brown

"Dogs love 'em," said the announcer. "The amazing Treat Timer. Treat your pet to Treat Timer. Only $19.95. Treats may vary. Batteries not included. If you love your pet—get a Treat Timer!"

"Wow!" said Arthur. "Pal needs one of those."

— From *Arthur's TV Trouble*, page 4

Thus begins *Arthur's TV Trouble*. Like so many young television viewers, Arthur hasn't learned that things aren't always as they appear on TV, and that sometimes Mother does know best—like when she says Pal probably would prefer to receive treats from Arthur instead of a machine.

But Arthur raids his piggybank, stacks newspapers for Mr. Sipple, and saves enough cash to buy Pal a treat timer. After five hours of arduous assembly, Pal runs for cover when the treats shoot out like rockets. Has Arthur learned his lesson, or will he get into more TV trouble?

Share the book for read-aloud, and then revisit the last page showing Arthur dreaming of D.W. inside the Magic Disappearing Box. Take a survey to find out the number of students who think Arthur will buy this newest invention from KidTricks.

Next let students get creative and make some inventions of their own, which will also help strengthen their fine-motor skills. Set up an area with various discarded items such as cardboard tubes from paper towel rolls, shoe boxes, foil pans, pipe cleaners, paper fasteners, wooden sticks, feathers, and so on.

After students make inventions that serve a purpose, have them share their creations with the class. Can they convince each other that their inventions are worth purchasing?

ON ANOTHER DAY

Set up an Invention Museum featuring your students' inventions. Put together a catalog with snapshots of each inventor and invention and a brief dictated description of his or her creation. Staple the pages together so the catalog can be perused at the silent reading library.

Rich Vocabulary

assembled *v.* put together

The Little Mouse, the Red Ripe Strawberry, and THE BIG HUNGRY BEAR
by Don and Audrey Wood

 **LEARNING ABOUT** **Pantomiming Actions**

Hello, little Mouse.
What are you doing?
Oh, I see.
Are you going to pick that red, ripe strawberry?
But, little Mouse,
haven't you heard about the big, hungry bear?

   — From *The Little Mouse, the Red Ripe Strawberry, and THE BIG HUNGRY BEAR*, pages 3–6

As the story continues, the narrator convinces little Mouse that the big hungry bear will find a red ripe strawberry that's just been picked no matter where it's hidden, disguised, or who guards it. The strawberry, incidentally, looks real enough to eat and may make readers want to rush off to buy a carton of fresh strawberries for themselves. Should readers fear a big hungry bear will eat their purchase? Or is someone else trying to get that red ripe strawberry?

The question for readers is who is actually interpreting Mouse's role. And who ultimately finagles half of the red ripe strawberry? Young readers are anxious to make predictions and request this story for read-aloud again and again. It has just enough drama and suspense to keep kindergartners on the edges of their seats for the first read-aloud, but it will get them out of their seats and moving for a book-based activity.

The favorite author team of Don and Audrey Wood has created a winning work that shows how Mouse's facial expressions and actions portray his feelings without a single word. Have students relate to Little Mouse's feelings in a pantomime that explores movement as a form of expression. Explain that pantomime is like a play where characters don't speak but instead perform the action. Emphasize to performers that Little Mouse's feelings must "speak" for themselves just as they do in Don Wood's illustrations. Take the role of the narrator, and read the story again.

> ### Rich Vocabulary
>
> **especially** *adv.*
> for a special reason

"Hello, little Mouse. What are you doing?"

Whistle for Willie
by Ezra Jack Keats

 **Listening Skills**

Peter saw his dog, Willie, coming.
Quick as a wink, he hid in an empty carton lying on the sidewalk.
"Wouldn't it be funny if I whistled?" Peter thought.
"Willie would stop and look all around to see who it was."
Peter tried again to whistle—but he still couldn't. So Willie just walked on.

— From *Whistle for Willie*, pages 10–11

> **Rich Vocabulary**
>
> **errand** *n.* a job that has to be done (such as mailing a letter)

Award-winning author Ezra Jack Keats celebrates the feeling of accomplishment young children feel when they conquer the art of whistling. "Lean down, Mommy," Ryan, my young son said after reading this book with me, "so I can whistle in your ear." Although I felt only the slightest breath and did not hear a sound, my son was thrilled with his newfound skill and rushed to whistle for his own dogs, Sydney and Jordan. Fortunately for Ryan, Sydney and Jordan were happy to see him and came running, whistle or not.

Let your young whistlers practice their whistling skills and boost their self-esteem through personal accomplishment with the following activity. Just as Peter hid in a box and tried to trick Willie by whistling for him, play a game with your students. Ask them to close their eyes. Tap a whistler on the shoulder to signal that it's his or her turn to hide (in a large box or elsewhere) while the rest of the class keeps their eyes closed. As the individual hidden in the box gives a whistle, the other students try to identify who it is.

If guesses are not accurate, tell students to open their eyes and, through the process of elimination, identify the person in the box. For non-whistlers, an instrument such as a kazoo can ease the no-whistle blues.

Even More Must-Have Books for Building Self-Esteem Through Art, Music, and Movement

Look Out Kindergarten, Here I Come by Nancy White Carlstrom

Gilberto and the Wind by Marie Hall Ets

The Painter by Peter Catalanotto

There's Something in the Attic by Mercer Mayer

The Trouble with Trolls by Jan Brett

Julius by Angela Johnson

Charlie Needs a Cloak by Tomie dePaola

Hattie and the Fox by Mem Fox

Snowballs by Lois Ehlert

Harold and the Purple Crayon by Crockett Johnson

The Little Engine that Could by Watty Piper

Rotten Ralph's Show and Tell by Jack Gantos

A Puppet Like Me!

Directions:
1. Make the puppet look like you!
2. Cut it out.
3. Glue the puppet to a stick.

Now you're ready to let off a little self-esteem!

Use with *I'm Gonna Like Me!* by Jamie Lee Curtis and Laura Cornell.

Chapter 5: Where the Wild Things Write

10 Must-Have Books for Responding to Literature

Chapter Learning Goals:

* using writing and other methods to describe familiar persons, places, objects, or experiences
* writing a story without words
* writing in a variety of forms or genres
* strengthening oral language skills by interpreting a story orally
* using letter-sound relationships in written compositions
* using describing words to tell a story
* making predictions about the events in a story

When I arrived to pick up my children from preschool one day, Ryan and Maddie were sitting with their friend, Jack, making shopping lists at the kitchen center.

"What else do we need from the store, Mom?" Ryan asked. "I already have waffles."

"Well, we're out of popcorn," I added. "P-P-P . . ."

"I have *p* for *popcorn*. Wait! There's the word *corn*!" Ryan pointed to a bulletin board with food words near the kitchen. "I'll copy that down. Just a few more things, and I'll be ready to go."

Ryan quickly reverted to scribble writing to finish his list. I was thrilled that he had taken the time and effort to sound-spell and was impressed with his results. When we got in the car, I gave him a pencil and asked him to add *cream* to his list.

"I wrote *cream* for you, Mommy." Maddie, my three-year-old, pointed to her own list of scribble writing and said, "Right here. And I wrote *ice cream*, too." She moved her finger down the list. "Right here."

"Oh, Maddie, that's wonderful! I'm impressed with the writing you two have done!" I was beaming with pride as I drove my two young writers to the store to pick up waffles, popcorn, cream, ice cream, and the other items on their lists.

Why am I telling you this story about my preschoolers in this book for kindergarten? Because Ryan and Maddie's enthusiasm for writing illustrates the importance of fun and practical first writing experiences, and because not all children have the experience of preschool. Kindergarten teachers are

> ## 10 Must-Have Books for Responding to Literature
>
> *Where the Wild Things Are* by Maurice Sendak
>
> *The Salamander Room* by Anne Mazer
>
> *A Boy, a Dog and a Frog* by Mercer Mayer
>
> *Timothy Goes to School* by Rosemary Wells
>
> *The Hat* by Jan Brett
>
> *Swimmy* by Leo Lionni
>
> *Imogene's Antlers* by David Small
>
> *Julius, the Baby of the World* by Kevin Henkes
>
> *In the Tall, Tall Grass* by Denise Fleming
>
> *Nana's Birthday Party* by Amy Hest

Teaching With Favorite Read-Alouds in Kindergarten

often the first teachers influencing a child's reading and writing efforts. It's the experiences and opportunities young children are presented with at the earliest stages of readiness that build confidence, lead to improvement, and turn them on to writing and reading.

The books and activities in this chapter will help young writers become "wild" about writing and reading. Tell stories with and without words like Maurice Sendak did in *Where the Wild Things Are*. Let imaginations and pencils run wild in *The Salamander Room*. Ask pairs of children to tell their versions of *A Boy, a Dog and a Frog*. Prove how pictures work with words with *Timothy Goes to School*. Predict what would happen next if the story of *The Hat* continued. Empower your children with sound-spelling confidence after reading *Swimmy* and *Imogene's Antlers*. Transform feelings into words with *Julius, the Baby of the World*. Put letters together to make words with *In the Tall, Tall Grass*. Get an idea down on paper so that it will never be forgotten for *Nana's Birthday Party*.

Inspire young writers with the great books in this chapter. Pass out sheets of paper, and watch the pages fill up with scribble writing, pictures to interpret orally, single letters that represent whole words, and sound-spelled words. The books on the following pages are perfect for getting kindergartners to write first responses to literature.

Ryan's list (age 5)

Maddie's list (age 3)

Where the Wild Things Are
by Maurice Sendak

LEARNING ABOUT Telling Stories Through Pictures

The night Max wore his wolf suit and made mischief
of one kind and another
his mother called him "WILD THING!"
and Max said "I'LL EAT YOU UP!"
so he was sent to bed without eating anything.
— From *Where the Wild Things Are*, pages 2–6

> **Rich Vocabulary**
>
> **mischief** *n.*
> annoying but harmless behavior

Where the Wild Things Are, the 1964 winner of the Caldecott Medal, is a classic book depicting what really happens when a little boy named Max is sent to his room. Max's creativity is unleashed when he puts on his wolf suit and becomes a mischievous wolf who uses a hammer and nails to build a den inside the house and chases the family dog with a fork.

This book is a favorite of young children who love entertaining thoughts of growing a forest in their room with an ocean and a boat just for them, sailing in and out of weeks to where the wild things are, and then being crowned King of the Wild Things. To young readers' delight, no words are needed to tell the story when the "wild rumpus starts" and, for the next six pages, Max and his wild friends howl at the moon, swing from the trees, and parade through the forest.

Use the award-winning and imagination-stirring illustrations in this book as a first-step introduction to writing. Your students will journey to where the wild things are for a mini-lesson that encourages telling stories through pictures and also shows how pictures and words work together to tell a story.

Gather boxes of crayons, sheets of paper, and a group of kindergartners with imaginations and take them to where the wild things write! Our mini-lesson begins as I read the page prior to the six wordless pages.

Mrs. L.:	"And now," cried Max, "let the wild rumpus start!" *(I share the illustrations without comment.)*
Jordan:	You didn't read that part.
Kelly:	There aren't any words to read.
Mrs. L.:	Tell about these pages and why Maurice Sendak didn't put any words on them.
Kyle:	Because the wild things' feet are in the way and everything else is, too. There wasn't room for words.
Renee:	He said so much in his drawings, he didn't need to write any words.
Mrs. L.:	Exactly! I think Maurice Sendak wanted the ideas inside Max and the wild things' minds to come from your imaginations.
Tara:	Or maybe they didn't say anything—they're just having fun!
Mrs. L.:	This is a very creative book with illustrations telling much of the story. Even the pages with words have very few words. Maurice Sendak won a very important award for this book. The award is called the Caldecott Medal. The Caldecott Medal is awarded to the book with the best pictures published that year. The first page of the book has a special page that reads, "Winner of the Caldecott Medal for the Most Distinguished Picture Book of the Year."
Paul:	That does sound special.
Mrs. L.:	It is one of the highest honors a writer or an illustrator can receive for a book. I bet the fact that children love *Where the Wild Things Are* is the best honor of all. This book is forty years old. My parents read this book to me, and now I read it to Ryan and Maddie and all of you! Let's talk a little bit about what makes these pictures award-winning and a favorite for so many years.
Jordan:	Well, he uses up all the white space like you always tell us to do.
Mrs. L.:	Yes, he does. Something I noticed is that as the forest grows in the story, so does the amount of space he uses to make the picture. Let me show you from the beginning. The first illustration of Max making mischief is drawn in a box surrounded by white space. The next page has a box that is a bit bigger. I'll keep turning the pages. Watch the illustration box get bigger and the white space gets smaller: "That very night in Max's room a forest grew . . ."
Wyatt:	The trees are growing outside the box on that page. Turn to the next page.
Tyler:	The box with the picture is BIGGER!
Mrs. L.:	I'll turn to the next page.
Class:	WOW!
Tyler:	It's the whole page.
Kevin:	No white at all!
Rebecca:	That took a lot of work.
Mrs. L.:	Listen to the words: ". . . and grew until his ceiling hung with vines and the walls became the world all around . . ."
Amy:	The picture is the whole page because it's the whole world around him.
Mrs. L.:	That's a great way to think of it. You have to look closely at pictures to make sure you are seeing everything the author wants you to see.
Andrew:	I want to be an artist when I grow up.

Rebecca:	Me, too.
Mrs. L.:	Well, I think looking closely at expert picture-makers is a great way to start. You can get so many ideas from looking at the pictures in books. As we said earlier, when a book's illustrations are as detailed as they are in *Where the Wild Things Are*, very few words are needed. Listen to the first page: "The night Max wore his wolf suit and made mischief of one kind . . ." These are the only words. Tell me something you know about the story just by looking at the picture.
Wyatt:	He's making a tent or a house for the bear.
Rebecca:	The bear's a "wild thing!"
Joni:	He's putting a nail in the wall—
Kevin:	That'll make his mom mad, I bet.
Tara:	He hung that bear there to make it look like the woods. And the string kind of looks like vines.
Tyler:	He's in his wolf suit so he's making the woods.
Mrs. L.:	Look at the next page. The only words are "and another." What do you see happening on the page?
Tara:	He's chasing his dog with a fork.
Kevin:	He's going to eat him since he's a wolf.
Paul:	I like the picture he drew of a wild thing. It's hanging on the wall.
Rebecca:	It shows what he's thinking about.
Joni:	And maybe when Max gets sent to his room, he falls asleep, and since he's thinking about being a wild wolf, the pictures aren't real, they're what he dreams.
Mrs. L.:	Good thinking. Look at Max's expression on the next page when he gets sent to his room.
Kyle:	He's mad. He was only playing wolf and he got sent to his room—
Joni:	—for using a hammer and nails and for chasing the dog with a fork.
Jordan:	I'd get in trouble for running with a fork even if I didn't chase our dog.
Renee:	There aren't any toys in the room for him to play with. There's only a bed so I bet he does fall asleep and dream.
Mrs. L.:	The first time I read *Where the Wild Things Are* for read-aloud, I almost missed one of the best parts. I was reading the ending where Max sails back over a year and in and out of weeks and through a day. *(I read page 38.)*: ". . . and into the night of his very own room where he found his supper waiting for him . . ."
Amy:	The end.
Mrs. L.:	That's what I thought. Luckily, I was curious to see if there was a picture of Max eating his supper or sleeping so I turned the page.
Brian:	No picture. Just words.
Mrs. L.:	Yes, and these are very special words: ". . . and it was still hot."
Kelly:	His supper was still hot.
Mrs. L.:	Maurice Sendak did extra work. He could have stopped writing on the page before. We know Max made it home safely and that his mother, even though she was disappointed in his behavior, saved dinner for him.

Kelly:	Since his dinner was still hot, he couldn't have been with the wild things for too long.
Kyle:	And, if his mother had brought his dinner to him and he wasn't in his room, she would have been worried and gone looking for him.
Tara:	She never would have known how to get to where the wild things are.
Mrs. L.:	I know Maurice Sendak would be thrilled that his book got your imaginations running as wild as Max's. Remember, illustrations tell something about the story that the words may not.
Joni:	Like that Max chased his dog with a fork.
Mrs. L.:	Exactly! Illustrations can also tell a story without words. Just like the wordless pages in *Where the Wild Things Are*, the pictures can tell the story without any words at all. Now it's time for your imaginations to run wild like the wild things. I want you to tell a story with pictures about Max and the wild things using all the white space—just like Maurice Sendak did.

Children may use crayons, colored pencils, or markers to make their own wild things creations on large sheets of white construction paper. During work time, I walk around, encouraging young artists to add details to *all* the white space. I offer assistance to those who want help sound-spelling words to describe their illustrations. When my young artists are finished, volunteers share their final products while their fellow author/illustrators offer words of praise and helpful suggestions. We proudly publish the masterpieces in the hall for all to see. Each piece displays a Room 4 Caldecott Medal, which I make out of shiny stickers.

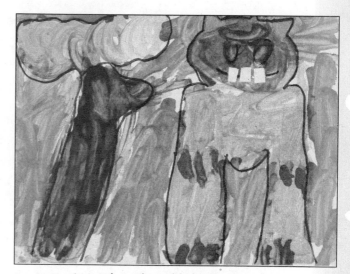

Inspiration from *Where the Wild Things Are*

TEACHING TIP

Introducing Sound-Spelling to Beginning Writers

Apply the technique used to introduce students to the way print is organized as an introduction to sound-spelling. Meet with individual students and ask each one to dictate a sentence to tell about their *Where the Wild Things Are* drawings. On the back of each illustration, draw a blank line for each word in the student's idea. Explain that each blank line is for one word in the idea. Together sound-spell the word for each blank line. Encourage students to record all of the sounds they hear in each word. For some students, the initial sound may represent the entire word.

Meet with one or two writers during writing time to help them break the task of writing into distinct units for sound-spelling.

More Must-Have Books for Responding to Literature

The Salamander Room
by Anne Mazer

LEARNING ABOUT **Strengthening Oral Language**

Brian found a salamander in the woods. It was a little orange salamander that crawled through the dried leaves of the forest floor.

The salamander was warm and cozy in the boy's hand. "Come live with me," Brian said.

He took the salamander home.

— From *The Salamander Room*, page 5

In this beautifully illustrated picture book, Brian's mother peppers her son with questions and comments about the decision to bring home the little salamander. Brian's imagination runs wild as he responds eloquently to each query and rather convincingly pleads his case for keeping his new friend, and each response leads to a natural follow-up from Mom.

The first time I shared this book with students, they sat mesmerized; they were convinced by Brian's eloquent ideas for keeping his unusual pet happy and hoping his mother would let him keep it. The ending leaves the final verdict up to readers; as Brian sleeps on his bed, covered with a blanket, his salamander sleeps at his bedside covered with a fresh green leaf. Is this Brian's imagination, or is the salamander his for keeps?

To further prove the power of illustrations, read *The Salamander Room* as a follow-up to *Where the Wild Things Are*. Reread Brian's mother's questions, and ask students to respond with their own convincing arguments. Have them search the illustrations for how Brian solved each potential problem from lack of friends to lack of food to too many insects.

ON ANOTHER DAY

Give students the opportunity to turn their bedrooms into a habitat for an unusual pet. Pass out sheets of white paper and colored pencils, markers, or crayons for them to illustrate the perfect sleeping space for their new pets. Remind students to keep food, sleeping, and animal friends in mind as they accommodate this space for themselves and their new pets.

Provide sharing time for students to convince their class-

Rich Vocabulary

boulder *n.* a large rock

mates that they should be able to keep their chosen pet in their rooms. Encourage them to include details in these explanations; Brian's salamander, for example, was a little orange salamander. Offer writing paper to those students who wish to include written descriptions with their illustrations.

....

A Boy, A Dog and a Frog
by Mercer Mayer

 **LEARNING ABOUT**

Interpreting Illustrations in a Story

For even more boy-and-his-pet fun, share this wordless book by Mercer Mayer, who proves he is a master at telling a story without words. As the boy and his dog set out to catch a frog, they fall in the pond and anger the frog before going home frog-less. The characters' facial expressions and the surprise ending make this a favorite of young readers. Best shared one-on-one or in a small group because of its size and detail, this must-have book empowers students to "read" independently. Every child can "read" each page and offer different interpretations and unique dialogue for the same sequence of events.

Read the title, and then show the first page. After a minute or two, turn the page. Continue in this manner for the entire book. As students comment, simply smile and continue displaying pages for them to view. After sharing the last page, close the book and say, "The end." Share the book a second time, asking for volunteers to "picture read" the pages.

MORE FUN WITH THE BOOK
During free time, invite pairs of students to take turns "reading" the words they would say for each page. Then meet with individuals so they can tell their versions to you. Oral retellings can be copied down word for word with the aid of a laptop computer and illustrated by each author.

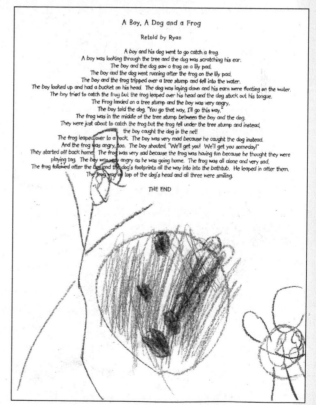

Ryan's version of *A Boy, a Dog and a Frog*

Rich Vocabulary

frustrated *v.* not being able to do something

Teaching With Favorite Read-Alouds in Kindergarten

Timothy Goes to School
by Rosemary Wells

Timothy's mother made him a brand-new sunsuit for the first day of school.
"Hooray!" said Timothy.
— From *Timothy Goes to School,* page 5

Introduce your illustration-savvy students to another master illustrator and favorite children's author, Rosemary Wells. The feelings of her characters are easily felt by readers; from a painful hair brushing on the title page to having Claude shatter Timothy's illusions of school to giggling so much that Timothy hiccups, readers relate to the range of emotions in this book.

Use the illustrations in this must-have book to put picture clues to the test. Begin by displaying the cover and asking children to make predictions about the story. Without reading the words, look at each page and encourage students to describe the events unfolding in the illustrations—as if the book were wordless. Skim the text on each page for words that are illustrated such as *pencil, puddle, saxophone*, and point out these objects to students. Young readers are relieved to realize that pictures often offer assistance for unknown words. With predictions in mind, reread *When Timothy Went to School*. Reinforce the points of the story that students accurately predicted and the events that were a surprise.

ON ANOTHER DAY

Following a rereading of the book, ask students to use a writer's perspective to discuss their favorite parts, what they might change in the story, or details they would add. Ask prospective writers about a story they would like to tell. Ideas might include the following:

• an event that happened at school
• a time they felt nervous about an upcoming event
• meeting a friend for the first time
• a time they laughed so hard they got the hiccups
• a time they wished someone would fall into a puddle

Encourage your young authors to use pictures, sound-spelling, or a combination of both to convey the ideas in their stories. Remind them to include as many clues about the story as possible. As students work, walk around the room to help individuals with spelling efforts. Be sure to end the activity with a sharing time where writers can receive feedback from the audience. Discuss problems, and share ideas for these works in progress. A few topics inspired by *Timothy Goes to School* are listed below.

W Brian Wt t Scr (When Brian Went to Soccer)
Wn Kelly mt Cr (When Kelly Met Cara)
Kyles sle dog z fne (Kyle's Silly Dog is Funny)

> ## Rich Vocabulary
>
> **supposed** *v.*
> expected

The Hat

by Jan Brett

LEARNING ABOUT Extending A Story

When curious Hedgie pokes his nose inside the woolen stocking that Lisa dropped, it gets stuck on his prickles. When the other animals see Hedgie, they laugh until he explains how warm and cozy he'll be in his new hat. Since Hedgie's pride keeps him from admitting that the stocking is stuck on his head, he continues to make excuses that plant ideas in the minds of the other animals. Each animal is inspired by Hedgie's new hat, and one by one Lisa's woolens mysteriously disappear from the clothesline.

Jan Brett uses border illustrations to keep readers anticipating the next story event. Lisa's activities are depicted on the left-hand border as she prepares for winter. The right-hand border foreshadows which animal will heckle Hedgie next. The border at the top shows the clothesline of Lisa's woolens. Page by page, different articles of clothing disappear as the animals fashion hats from them; Lisa's gloves fit the hen, a woolen vest warms the pig's ears, a scarf makes a perfect head covering for the cat, and so on. To young children, exploring the borders and discerning their inherent pattern is as much fun as the main plot.

Kick off a writing activity by giving your students practice in extending the story. Following a read-aloud of *The Hat*, reread the last page: *Lisa was still chasing them when Hedgie reached his den. "How ridiculous they look! Don't they know that animals should never wear clothes!"*

Challenge students to tell what happens next with the following suggestion: What if we turned the page, and there was more writing? What do you think would happen next? After students make their predictions, close the book and show them the basket filled with woolens on the back cover. (One perceptive student explained that this basket must hold the items Lisa gathered from the animals since there was snow on the ground under the basket and it didn't start snowing until after the animals began taking Lisa's things.) Pass out paper for students to record their ideas of what happens next using illustrations, including borders, and sound-spelling.

MORE FUN WITH THE BOOK

Set up a center where students can retell the story using paper cutouts or real clothing to represent the clothing from the story. Place an audiotape of *The Hat* in the center also so pairs of students can remove each item of clothing from a clothesline hanging in the center.

> ## Rich Vocabulary
>
> **startled** *v.* surprised
>
> **ridiculous** *adj.* very funny or silly

Swimmy
by Leo Lionni

LEARNING ABOUT
Writing Descriptions

To explore how pictures and words work together, share Leo Lionni's story about the smart little fish who isn't about to spend his life hiding from big fish. This Caldecott Honor book is perfect for exploring a simple but impressive illustrating technique as Swimmy and his new friends use the power of illustration to scare away the bigger fish. Read and discuss the eloquent words as the lonely little Swimmy explores the sea alone after his family is eaten by bigger fish.

Let your students reproduce the picture of Swimmy and his friends on pages 28–29 of the book using potato or sponge prints. Prior to the activity, outline a simple fish on a potato half or a sponge and cut away the outer edges to make a stamp. (You may enlarge the sample shape shown at the right.)

Hang a large sheet of butcher block paper. With a pencil, lightly draw the outline of a large fish. One by one, have students fill in the large fish outline with small fish using their stamps dipped in orange paint. Trace and cut out one more little fish from black construction paper to represent Swimmy, the eye of the giant orange fish.

While individuals take turns painting, pass out sentence strips to the rest of the class on which students can sound-spell or dictate a description of their illustrations of Swimmy on this class mural.

Swimmy outline

Swimmy and his friends

Rich Vocabulary

swift *adj.* quick, fast

Teaching With Favorite Read-Alouds in Kindergarten

Imogene's Antlers
by David Small

LEARNING ABOUT

Writing Stories

On Thursday, when Imogene woke up, she found she had grown antlers.
— From *Imogene's Antlers*, page 5

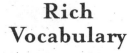
Rich Vocabulary

glared *v.* stared at in a mean way

advice *n.* words you say to help someone with a problem

Although getting dressed, going down to breakfast, and leaving through the front door presented some problems for Imogene and her antlers, there were a few perks to her newfound predicament. Mrs. Perkins, the cook, "decked her out" with doughnuts and sent her into the garden to feed the birds; she also thought Imogene would be lots of fun to decorate for Christmas. Imogene's mother's response, however, was to faint upon seeing Imogene's antlers. After holding a family meeting, it was decided that Imogene's antlers must be hidden under a hat. The result once again caused Mother to faint. In the end, the hat proved unnecessary when Imogene woke up antler-less the next day. Besides, a hat could do nothing to hide the peacock feathers she had grown instead!

After our first read-aloud of this book, I ask the children: "What if you woke up and found you had grown antlers during the night? Or peacock feathers? Or something else?" Let *Imogene's Antlers* get young imaginations running wild as the possible plights and potential perks of each scenario are envisioned.

Then get pencils moving with a giggle-filled creative writing lesson inspired by *Imogene's Antlers!* Jot down story starter ideas. Here are some examples I've used.

What If You Woke Up and Found You . . .
- *had grown into a giant . . . or had shrunk?*
- *had turned invisible during the night?*
- *had turned into a donkey or another animal with four legs?*
- *had grown a tail or a snout or a bill or feathers?*
- *barked every time you tried to talk?*

Ask students to choose an idea to write and illustrate. As they work, urge them to talk about their stories. Walk around the room, and encourage sound-spelling of at least one idea for each student. Be sure to provide a sharing time where students proudly display their what-if stories.

I sneak candy. I'm invisible.

Julius, the Baby of the World
by Kevin Henkes

Writing About Experiences

Before Julius was born, Lilly was the best big sister in the world.
She gave him things.
She told him secrets.
And she sang lullabies to him every night.
After Julius was born, it was a different story . . .
. . . "I am the queen," said Lilly. "And I hate Julius."
— From *Julius, the Baby of the World*, pages 5–6

Kevin Henke's honest portrayal of Lilly's feelings when her new baby brother steals the show from her, queen of the family, offers comfort to young readers in a similar situation. Whether it's Lilly's realization that Julius will not be leaving, the increasing amount of time she spends in the uncooperative chair, Cousin Garland's insult, or a combination of all three, Lilly has a change of heart with regard to baby Julius. As Lilly's open hatred for her new baby brother turns into protective and fierce love, her days of tail pinching and yelling insults into Julius's crib are replaced with kissing, admiring, and stroking.

After reading the story, use tell-me questions such as the following to stimulate a book-talk of *Julius, the Baby of the World* that will get your kindergartners writing about their own insecurities, experiences, and secret wishes.

Tell Me About . . .
- *a time you wished you could change something that couldn't be changed*
- *a time you felt like a queen or a king*
- *how Julius must have felt when Lilly pinched, insulted, or frightened him*
- *how you think Lilly felt in her heart when she did these things to Julius*
- *Lilly's story entitled "Julius, the Germ of the World"*
- *Lilly's glorious dreams and ghastly nightmares*
- *the picture Lilly made of her "entire complete family" showing Lilly, her mom, and her dad—and the words "that's all there is really."*
- *what happened when cousin Garland said unkind things about Julius*
- *a time you defended a sibling or friend*
- *the happy ending*

Rich Vocabulary

admired *v.* looked at with love

extraordinary *adj.* very special

Reread page 18 where Lilly tells Julius her story, "The Germ of the World"—the story that earned her ten extra minutes in the uncooperative chair. Pass out story writing paper for students to "write a story" inspired by *Julius, the Baby of the World*. Remind them that pictures alone, pictures with sound-spelling or dictated words, and pictures explained aloud are all ways of "writing a story."

···

In the Tall, Tall Grass
by Denise Fleming

LEARNING ABOUT **Descriptive Language**

Read the poetic and rhyming word story told by Denise Fleming to introduce students to descriptive words. As the little yellow caterpillar crawls across each page of the book, he relates sights and sounds with great rhyming words that make a memorable description of his journey. First, read the story and talk about how effective Denise Fleming's words are for describing what animals do in the tall, tall grass.

Then compare her word choices with less exciting words that she could have written to mean the same thing, such as the following:

> *Caterpillars eat.*
> *Bees buzz.*
> *A blackbird flies.*
> *Ants pull.*
> *Snakes crawl.*

My students agree that crunching and munching lunch is more exciting than just eating lunch. Give beginning writers a chance to explore writing with descriptive language by growing a tall grass zoo of describing words.

Pass out green construction paper, and direct students to cut fringe for grass

A snake is slithering with a caterpillar.

Rich Vocabulary

scurry *v.* to move quickly

swoop *v.* to dip down from above

---

that will be glued onto a background color of their choice. Next have them draw or cut and paste a caterpillar exploring in the tall, tall grass. What animal does their caterpillar encounter? They can add this creature to the illustration. Assist students in sound-spelling words that describe the sound their animal makes in the tall, tall grass.

ON ANOTHER DAY

Rhyming Words: Copy families of rhyming words from the story onto sentence strips in two contrasting colors—for example, red for the beginning letter(s), black for the rhyming chunk of the word. Tuck pairs of rhyming words, a few at a time, in scrambled order among blades of construction-paper grass attached to a bulletin board. Let pairs of students work together to match the rhyming word pairs by identifying the same letters shared by each pair. Or have them listen to *In the Tall, Tall Grass* on tape and stop the recording to arrange the rhyming word pairs from the bulletin board in order.

Nana's Birthday Party
by Amy Hest

LEARNING ABOUT **Writing Stories**

Brette and Maggie don't know what to make for Nana's birthday present. Then Nana gets her hatbox of photos that's "more fun than a box of candy," and the three of them sit close together on the big old couch.

> *"Remember," Nana says, "every picture tells a story."*
> *Brette holds up a yellowed one with curling edges.*
> *"What's the story here?" she asks.*
> — From *Nana's Birthday Party*, page 23

After hearing stories about their mothers when they were little girls, Brette sets up her easel and begins to paint a picture that's "better even than some grown-ups," while Maggie begins to "weave words into sentences that are lovely to read." Together the two cousins make Nana the grandest birthday present ever.

Following your read-aloud of the book, send a note home with students asking them to bring in a photo to write about (don't forget to bring in one of your own favorite photos, too). Gather students and their snapshots for an introductory activity on recording a story in words and pictures so it will never be forgotten. Remind your budding writers that "every picture tells a story."

Rich Vocabulary

occasion *n.* a special event

finest *adj.* best

Using your own snapshot as an example, verbally tell students the story and then transfer one idea from your verbal tale into print. To introduce sound-spelling, ask for assistance in writing down the main sounds in each of the words. As students share their photos one at a time, help them identify one sentence "that should never be forgotten." Pass out paper so they can illustrate their snapshots with drawings. Have them write at least one memorable idea (or more)—just as Maggie and Brette did for Nana. Encourage young writers with a reminder that even though the words may not look exactly like the words in a book, they will be able to share the story with others. This encouragement can be motivating for beginning writers.

Even More Must-Have Books for Responding to Literature

The Stray Dog by Marc Simont

The Kissing Hand by Audrey Penn

Peter's Chair by Ezra Jack Keats

Much Bigger Than Martin by Steven Kellogg

If You Give a Mouse a Cookie by Laura Jeff Numeroff

The Giving Tree by Shel Silverstein

The Snow Child by Debi Gliori

Truelove by Babette Cole

Imagine by Alison Lester

The Snow Speaks by Nancy White Carlstrom

Hedgie's Surprise by Jan Brett

50 Must-Have Books for Kindergarten

Asch, Frank. *Happy Birthday, Moon*. New York: Simon & Schuster, 1982.

Brett, Jan. *The Hat*. New York: G.P. Putnam's Sons, 1997.

Brown, Marc. *Arthur's TV Trouble*. Boston: Little, Brown & Company, 1995.

Burton, Virginia Lee. *Katy and the Big Snow*. Boston: Houghton Mifflin Company, 1943.

Cabrera, Jan. *Over in the Meadow*. New York: Holiday House, 1999.

Carle, Eric. *From Head to Toe*. New York: Harper Collins Publishers, Inc., 1997.

———. *Today Is Monday*. New York: Scholastic, Inc., 1993.

Christelow, Eileen. *Five Little Monkeys Jumping on the Bed*. New York: Clarion Books, 1989.

Curtis, Jamie Lee and Cornell, Laura. *I'm Gonna Like Me*. New York: HarperCollins Publishers, 2002.

Ehlert, Lois. *Eating the Alphabet: Fruits and Vegetables from A to Z*. New York: Voyager Books, 1989.

———. *Top Cat*. New York: Harcourt Brace & Company, 1998.

Falconer, Ian. *Olivia Saves the Circus*. New York: Atheneum Books for Young Readers, 2001.

Fleming, Denise. *Alphabet Under Construction*. New York: Henry Holt and Company, 2002.

———. *In the Tall, Tall Grass*. New York: Henry Holt and Company, 1991.

Garcia, Jerry. *The Teddy Bears' Picnic*. New York: HarperCollins Publishers, Inc., 1996.

Geisel, Theodore (Dr. Seuss). *The Cat in the Hat*. New York: Random House, 1957.

Hague, Kathleen. *Alphabears*. New York: Henry Holt and Company, Inc., 1984.

Henkes, Kevin. *Julius, the Baby of the World*. New York: Greenwillow Books, 1990.

———. *Sheila Rae, the Brave*. New York: Viking Penguin, 1987.

Hest, Amy. *Nana's Birthday Party*. New York: Morrow Junior Books, 1993.

Hillenbrand, Will. *Down by the Station*. Orlando: Harcourt Brace & Company, 1999.

Hoberman, Mary Ann. *The Eensy-Weensy Spider*. New York: Little, Brown and Company, 2000.

———. *One of Each*. New York: Little, Brown and Company, 1997.

Keats, Ezra Jack. *Whistle for Willie*. New York: Viking Children's Books, 1964.

Kellogg, Steven. *Give the Dog a Bone*. New York: SeaStar Books, 2000.

———. *The Missing Mitten Mystery*. New York: Dial Books for Young Readers, 2000.

Lionni, Leo. *Inch by Inch*. New York: William Morrow & Co., 1960.

———. *Swimmy*. New York: Alfred A. Knopf, Inc., 1963.

Martin, Bill, Jr. and Archambault, John. *Polar Bear, Polar Bear, What Do You Hear?* New York: Henry Holt and Company, 1991.

Mayer, Mercer. *A Boy, A Dog and A Frog*. New York: Dial Books for Young Readers, 1967.

Mazer, Anne. *The Salamander Room*. New York: Alfred A. Knopf, Inc., 1991.

McCloskey, Robert. *Blueberries for Sal*. New York: Puffin Books, 1948.

———. *Make Way for Ducklings*. New York: The Viking Press, 1941.

Merriam, Eve. *12 Ways to Get to 11*. New York: Simon & Schuster Books for Young Readers, 1993.

Munsch, Robert. *Purple, Green and Yellow*. New York: Annick Press Ltd., 1992.

Murphy, Stuart J. *A Pair of Socks*. New York: HarperCollins Publishers, 1996.

Raffi. *Wheels on the Bus*. New York: Crown Publishers, Inc., 1988.

Riley, Linnea. *Mouse Mess*. New York: The Blue Sky Press, 1997.

Rylant, Cynthia. *The Cookie-Store Cat*. New York: The Blue Sky Press, 1999.

Sendak, Maurice. *Chicken Soup with Rice*. New York: HarperCollins Publishers, Inc., 1962.

———. *Where the Wild Things Are*. New York: Harper Collins Publishers, Inc., 1963.

Slate, Joseph. *Miss Bindergarten Celebrates the 100th Day of Kindergarten*. New York: Puffin Books, 1998.

Slobodkina, Esphyr. *Caps for Sale*. New York: HarperCollins Publishers, 1940.

Small, David. *Imogene's Antlers*. New York: Crown Publishers, Inc., 1985.

Trapani, Iza. *Twinkle, Twinkle, Little Star*. Watertown, Maine: Charlesbridge Publishing.

Wells, Rosemary. *Bunny Money*. New York: Dial Books for Young Readers, 1997.

———. *Timothy Goes to School*. New York: Penguin Putnam Books for Young Readers, 1981.

Wescott, Nadine Bernard. *The Lady with the Alligator Purse*. New York: Little, Brown & Company, 1988.

Williams, Vera B. *Music, Music for Everyone*. New York: Greenwillow Books, 1984.

Wood, Don and Wood, Audrey. *The Little Mouse, The Red Ripe Strawberry, and THE BIG HUNGRY BEAR*. Wiltshire, England: Child's Play International, 1984.

Kindergarten Learning Skills

READING AND WRITING

Beginning letter sounds
Mouse Mess, pp. 16–17

Enhancing fluency
Over in the Meadow, pp. 28–29

Letter-sound relationships
Alphabet under Construction,
pp. 14–16
*Polar Bear, Polar Bear, What Do
You Hear?*, pp. 13–14

Letter and name recognition
Alphabears, pp. 18–19

Letter and word recognition
Down by the Station, pp. 30–31
Give the Dog a Bone, pp. 33–34
Today Is Monday, pp. 34–35
Twinkle, Twinkle, Little Star,
pp. 29–30
Wheels on the Bus, pp. 31–32

Organizing letters and words
The Cookie-Store Cat, pp. 21–22

Print organization
Sheila Rae, the Brave, pp. 20–21

Reading strategies
Interpreting illustrations in a story:
A Boy, a Dog and a Frog, p. 85
Making predictions:
Timothy Goes to School, p. 86
Sequencing:
Down by the Station, pp. 30–31
The Eensy Weensy Spider,
pp. 25–27
The Teddy Bears' Picnic, pp. 37–38

Sound-spelling
Nana's Birthday Party, pp. 92–93
Olivia Saves the Circus, pp. 19–20
Swimmy, p. 88
Twinkle, Twinkle, Little Star,
pp. 29–30
Where the Wild Things Are,
pp. 80–83

Speaking and listening skills
A Boy, a Dog and a Frog, p. 85
Caps for Sale, pp. 70–71
*Five Little Monkeys Jumping on the
Bed*, pp. 32–33
The Salamander Room, pp. 84–85
Whistle for Willie, p. 76

Vocabulary awareness
Sight words:
The Lady with the Alligator Purse,
pp. 35–36
Identifying days of the week:
Today Is Monday, pp. 34–35
Identifying fruits and vegetables:
*Eating the Alphabet: Fruits and
Vegetables from A to Z*,
pp. 17–18
Rhyming words:
The Cat in the Hat, pp. 8–12
In the Tall, Tall Grass, pp. 91–92
Top Cat, pp. 22–23

Writing
Descriptive language:
In the Tall, Tall Grass, pp. 91–92
Swimmy, p. 88
Extending a story:
The Hat, p. 87
Telling stories through pictures
Where the Wild Things Are,
pp. 80–83
Stories:
A Boy, a Dog and a Frog, p. 85
Imogene's Antlers, p. 89
Julius, the Baby of the World,
pp. 90–91
Nana's Birthday Party, pp. 92–93
Timothy Goes to School, p. 86

MATH

Addition and subtraction
Blueberries for Sal, pp. 55–56

Counting
Blueberries for Sal, pp. 55–56
Bunny Money, pp. 45–48
*Miss Bindergarten Celebrates the
100th Day of Kindergarten*,
pp. 50–51

Equal parts
One of Each, pp. 53–54

Estimation
Blueberries for Sal, pp. 55–56

Measuring length
Inch by Inch, pp. 57–58

Money
Bunny Money, pp. 45–48

Number sense
12 Ways to Get to 11, pp. 52–53

Patterns
A Pair of Socks, pp. 58–59
Katy and the Big Snow, pp. 59–60

Problem solving
The Missing Mitten Mystery,
pp. 56–57

Time (months/calendars)
Chicken Soup with Rice, pp. 49–50

PERSONAL GROWTH

Celebrating personal strengths
*I'm Gonna Like Me: Letting Off a
Little Self-Esteem*, pp. 64–67

Self-expression
Art:
Happy Birthday, Moon, p. 70
Purple, Green and Yellow, p. 68
Making inventions:
Arthur's TV Trouble, p. 74
Movement:
Caps for Sale, pp. 70–71
From Head to Toe, pp. 71–73
Make Way for Ducklings, p. 69
Music:
Make Way for Ducklings, p. 69
Music, Music for Everyone, p. 73
Pantomime:
*The Little Mouse, the Red Ripe
Strawberry, and THE BIG
HUNGRY BEAR*, p. 75